ASCENT
CENTER FOR TECHNICAL KNOWLEDGE

Autodesk® Showcase® 2017 (R1) Fundamentals

Student Guide
1ˢᵗ Edition

AUTODESK.
Authorized Publisher

ASCENT - Center for Technical Knowledge®
Autodesk® Showcase® 2017 (R1)
Fundamentals
1st Edition

Prepared and produced by:

ASCENT Center for Technical Knowledge
630 Peter Jefferson Parkway, Suite 175
Charlottesville, VA 22911

866-527-2368
www.ASCENTed.com

Lead Contributor: Renu Muthoo

ASCENT - Center for Technical Knowledge is a division of Rand Worldwide, Inc., providing custom developed knowledge products and services for leading engineering software applications. ASCENT is focused on specializing in the creation of education programs that incorporate the best of classroom learning and technology-based training offerings.

We welcome any comments you may have regarding this student guide, or any of our products. To contact us please email: feedback@ASCENTed.com.

AS-SHC1701-FND1NU-SG   //   IS-SHC1701-FND1NU-SG

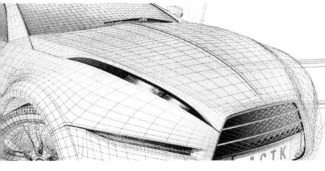

Contents

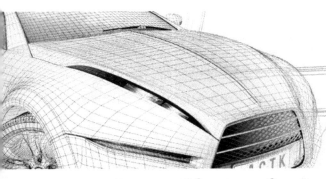

Preface

The *Autodesk® Showcase® 2017 (R1) Fundamentals* student guide instructs students in how to use the visualization and presentation tools in the Autodesk Showcase software to create compelling presentations of 3D CAD data. In the practice- intensive curriculum, students acquire the knowledge required to progress from importing data for use in a scene, preparing it for presentation, and publishing it as an image or movie or in a web presentation format.

Topics include:

- Overview of the Autodesk Showcase interface and workflow
- Importing Models
- Opening scenes
- Adjusting surface normal
- Selecting and transforming objects
- Assigning visual styles to enhance a scene
- Setting and manipulating rendering styles
- Adding lighting and shadow environments
- Adding accent lights to a scene
- Adding materials to objects in a scene
- Creating and manipulating design alternatives
- Creating and manipulating cross-sections
- Creating and manipulating Shots
- Creating and manipulating Behaviors
- Creating a Storyboard to present a scene
- Using the Pointer Tool to focus attention on a specific area
- Compare Scenes by placing two scenes side-by-side
- Publishing images, movies, and web presentations

Note on Software Setup

This student guide assumes a standard installation of the software using the default preferences during installation. Lectures and practices use the standard software templates and default options for the Content Libraries.

Students and Educators can Access Free Autodesk Software and Resources

Autodesk challenges you to get started with free educational licenses for professional software and creativity apps used by millions of architects, engineers, designers, and hobbyists today. Bring Autodesk software into your classroom, studio, or workshop to learn, teach, and explore real-world design challenges the way professionals do.

Get started today - register at the Autodesk Education Community and download one of the many Autodesk software applications available.

Visit www.autodesk.com/joinedu/

Note: Free products are subject to the terms and conditions of the end-user license and services agreement that accompanies the software. The software is for personal use for education purposes and is not intended for classroom or lab use.

Lead Contributor: Renu Muthoo

Renu uses her instructional design training to develop courseware for AutoCAD and AutoCAD vertical products, Autodesk 3ds Max, Autodesk Showcase and various other Autodesk software products. She has worked with Autodesk products for the past 20 years with a main focus on design visualization software.

Renu holds a bachelor's degree in Computer Engineering and started her career as a Instructional Designer/Author where she co-authored a number of Autodesk 3ds Max and AutoCAD books, some of which were translated into other languages for a wide audience reach. In her next role as a Technical Specialist at a 3D visualization company, Renu used 3ds Max in real-world scenarios on a daily basis. There, she developed customized 3D web planner solutions to create specialized 3D models with photorealistic texturing and lighting to produce high quality renderings.

Renu Muthoo has been the Lead Contributor for *Autodesk Showcase Fundamentals* since its initial release in 2013.

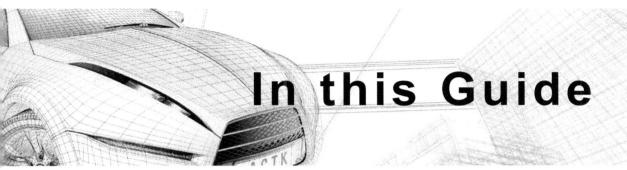

In this Guide

The following images highlight some of the features that can be found in this Student Guide.

Practice Files

The Practice Files page tells you how to download and install the practice files that are provided with this student guide.

FTP link for practice files

Chapters

Each chapter begins with a brief introduction and a list of the chapter's Learning Objectives.

Learning Objectives for the chapter

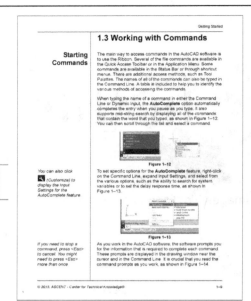

Instructional Content

Each chapter is split into a series of sections of instructional content on specific topics. These lectures include the descriptions, step-by-step procedures, figures, hints, and information you need to achieve the chapter's Learning Objectives.

Side notes

Side notes are hints or additional information for the current topic.

Practice Objectives

Practices

Practices enable you to use the software to perform a hands-on review of a topic.

Some practices require you to use prepared practice files, which can be downloaded from the link found on the Practice Files page.

Chapter Review Questions

Chapter review questions, located at the end of each chapter, enable you to review the key concepts and learning objectives of the chapter.

Command Summary

The Command Summary is located at the end of each chapter. It contains a list of the software commands that are used throughout the chapter, and provides information on where the command is found in the software.

Practice Files

To download the practice files for this student guide, use the following steps:

1. Type the URL shown below into the address bar of your Internet browser. The URL must be typed **exactly as shown**. If you are using an ASCENT ebook, you can click on the link to download the file.

Address bar

http://www.ASCENTed.com/getfile?id=accipitridae

File   Edit   View   Favorites   Tools   Help

2. Press <Enter> to download the .ZIP file that contains the Practice Files.

3. Once the download is complete, unzip the file to a local folder. The unzipped file contains an .EXE file.

4. Double-click on the .EXE file and follow the instructions to automatically install the Practice Files on the C:\ drive of your computer.

   Do not change the location in which the Practice Files folder is installed. Doing so can cause errors when completing the practices in this student guide.

http://www.ASCENTed.com/getfile?id=accipitridae

Stay Informed!

Interested in receiving information about upcoming promotional offers, educational events, invitations to complimentary webcasts, and discounts? If so, please visit:

www.ASCENTed.com/updates/

Help us improve our product by completing the following survey:

www.ASCENTed.com/feedback

You can also contact us at: *feedback@ASCENTed.com*

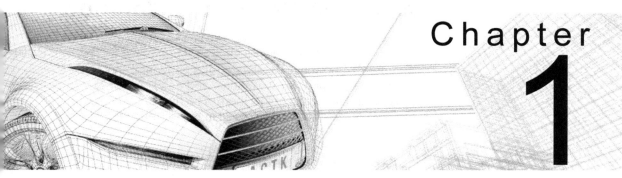

Chapter 1

Introduction to Autodesk Showcase

In this chapter you learn how to plan your presentation projects, start the Autodesk® Showcase® software, and become familiar with the basic layout of the interface. You also learn to import files, save the files, and open the 3D scene files.

Learning Objectives in this Chapter

- Identify the various data sources that can be brought into the Autodesk Showcase software.
- Plan your presentation projects using the common workflow process.
- Work with the model and navigate around the scene using the various interface components and tools.
- Import 3D CAD data files and control the import settings.
- Review and modify the import status of the files.
- Save the 3D CAD data file and open the scene files in the software.

Autodesk Showcase Workflow

Figure 1–1 shows the overall suggested workflow for the Autodesk® Showcase® software. The horizontal line at the top represents the high-level workflow and each of their sub-steps are detailed vertically below them. The highlighted column represents the content discussed in the current chapter.

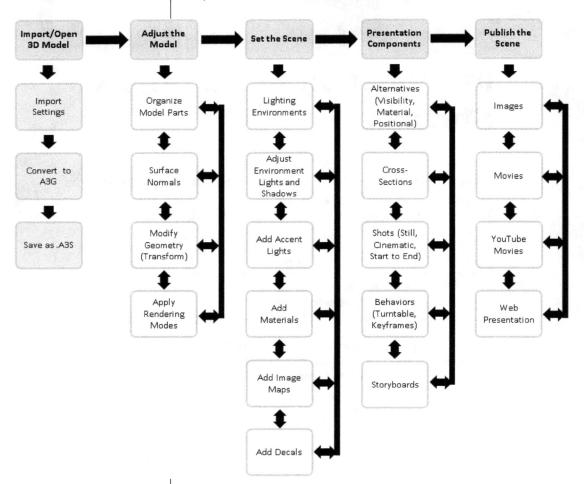

Figure 1–1

1.1 Overview

The Autodesk Showcase software is a visualization, presentation, and communication package used in the design presentation of 3D CAD data.

- It is used to create high quality single-frame still imagery of virtually any size, including large-format presentation graphics, enabling you to transform your CAD geometry into movies and real-time presentations.

- It is used to create different variations of a component or product in the form of different backgrounds, materials, lighting, and positions with interactive renderings of these variation.

- You can then assemble these variations and present them as design prototypes or marketing material.

*A free application, **Autodesk Showcase Viewer is** provided by Autodesk that enables you to view and navigate the scenes created by the Autodesk Showcase software.*

- It can be used by designers, engineers, and marketing professionals to create high quality renderings of 3D CAD designs and to present and communicate the designs easily and effectively. Figure 1–2 shows a rendering of a building in the Autodesk Showcase software.

Figure 1–2

File Compatibility

An Autodesk Showcase .A3S file is referred to as a *scene* file.

The Autodesk Showcase software comes with the Autodesk® DirectConnect software installed automatically. The Autodesk DirectConnect software is a file translator that converts all of the imported CAD data to Autodesk Packet Files (APF) that are read by the Autodesk Showcase software.

Input into Autodesk Showcase

The Autodesk Showcase software is not a 3D modeling tool, so you need to import 3D CAD data from other 3D data creation software. A number of 3D CAD data files can be imported into the Autodesk Showcase software from multiple data sources, including:

- AutoCAD® drawing files (.DWG and .DXF), including objects created in vertical applications, such as the AutoCAD® Architecture software.

- Autodesk® Revit® Architecture designs are imported directly into the Autodesk Showcase software.

- Autodesk® Inventor® files (.IPT and .IAM) can be directly imported into the Autodesk Showcase software and all of the Autodesk Inventor constraints can be translated into behaviors.

- Autodesk® Alias® .Wire files.

- Autodesk® Simulation designs are imported into the Autodesk Showcase software as exported .FBX files.

- Other major CAD data applications, such as CATIA, Creo Elements/Pro, SolidWorks, STEP, IGES, and Stl files.

- Autodesk® Maya® and Autodesk® 3ds Max® animations can be brought and played in the Autodesk Showcase software.

1.2 Workflow Process

Each presentation project can be very different from the next, but most follow a common general workflow. The default settings of the tools are geared toward the work that might be done in architectural, mechanical, or civil visualizations. Figure 1–3 shows a suggested approach to help plan your design visualization and presentation projects.

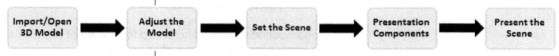

Figure 1–3

Import/Open a File

The first step in creating your visualization design is to import the required 3D CAD geometry. 3D CAD data is available from other design software, such as Autodesk Inventor, AutoCAD, Autodesk Revit, CATIA, IGES etc. Before importing the CAD data do the following:

- Prepare the models in the originating software with the intent of importing them into Autodesk Showcase software by limiting the number of polygons, objects, and materials.

- After designing the model or geometry, you can directly launch and open the scene from specific Autodesk software, such as Autodesk Inventor, AutoCAD, Autodesk Revit, and Autodesk Alias. This enables you to keep the link between the models active so that changes made in the originating software are reflected.

Adjust the Models

After converting he geometry, adjust it by modifying the settings and fixing any bad imported data.

- Verify that the surface normals are facing the right direction and modify their direction as required.

- If the geometry looks jagged, you might need to modify the Level of Detail (LOD) settings for the models. If you increase the LOD settings, the speed and performance might be affected.

Set the Scene

The next step is to set the scene. You might need to import additional geometry from other files, hide geometry that might not be required, add environments, and add ambient shadows. This could also involve adjusting the materials, lights, and shadows to achieve the required results.

Presentation Components

For presenting you can:

- Create visibility, material, and/or positional alternatives for different variations of the model.

- Add cross-sectional views and exploded views of the part to present internal configurations of the model.

- Set up shots to create single-frame still renderings or moving shots with cinematic camera movement.

- Add behaviors to create animations of the models.

- Create Storyboards using an environment and add shots, alternatives, and behaviors.

Publish the Scene

Finally, to present your scene you can:

- Create a movie by compiling the shots and slides together.

- Create a walkthrough using your SteeringWheel and present it interactively.

- Publish the images, movies, and animations to the web, YouTube, or a mobile device.

1.3 Autodesk Showcase Interface

To launch the Autodesk Showcase software, use one of the following methods:

- Double-click on 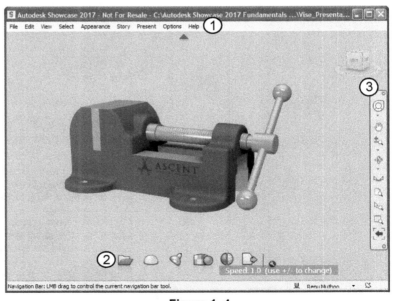 (Autodesk Showcase 2017) on your desktop.

- From the **Start** button in the Windows Task Bar, select **All Programs>Autodesk>Autodesk Showcase 2017> Showcase 2017**.

When you launch the software for the first time, a Welcome screen displays where you can watch short videos that teach you essential skills and concepts about the software. Click **Close** to start working in the interface. You can open the Welcome screen at anytime by selecting **Help>Learning Movies** in the Menu Bar.

The Autodesk Showcase viewport with the interface features displays. In the example shown in Figure 1–4, a 3D model of a vise is opened to display some of the interface elements.

Figure 1–4

1. Main Menu

The Menu Bar displays on top of the Autodesk Showcase viewport and contains menus for accessing the Autodesk Showcase commands. The Menu Bar is hidden when you launch the software for the first time.

The display of the Main Menu is also controlled in the Task UI by

clicking ◉ and selecting **Show Menu Bar***.*

Click ▼ at the top of the viewport window to open the Menu Bar. This icon toggles to ▲ when the Menu Bar displays. Working commands are grouped together in each of the menu titles, as shown in Figure 1–5 for the **File** menu.

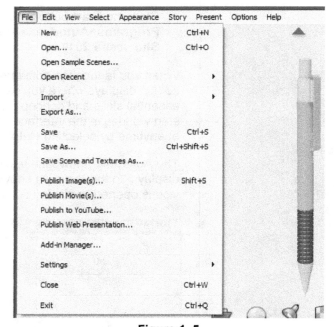

Figure 1–5

The available menus are described as follows:

File	Contains the **New**, **Open**, **Import**, **Close**, and **Save** commands in addition to the **Publish** commands. It also contains the different options for changing the Settings.
Edit	Contains commands to undo, duplicate, and delete functions. It also contains commands for fixing the normals and patches in the geometry.
View	Contains features to display the views and controls for displaying the navigation tools.

Select	Contains the various object selection and hide/unhide options.
Appearance	Contains options that enable you to control the appearance of your 3D data. These enable you to work with the materials, lighting, and shadows on an object, ray tracing, and visual styles.
Story	Contains features used for creating the components of a presentation, such as Alternatives, Behaviors, Shots, and a Storyboard.
Present	Contains comparison features, collaboration mode, and presentation mode commands.
Options	Contains toggles for controlling the display of grips (handles) for various features, such as Accent light, Cross-Section, and Decal. It also contains toggles for displaying the Task UI, Trigger notification, and options for other display features.
Help	Contains the Autodesk Showcase Help documentation and other features, such as Message Reference, Keyboard Shortcuts, etc. It also contains other options that connect you to the online Autodesk Showcase services and supports at the autodesk.com website.

2. Task UI

The Task UI (as shown in Figure 1–6) displays at the bottom of the Autodesk Showcase viewport and enables you to easily access the main features used for creating highly realistic images, movies, and presentations. By default, the Task UI displays in the viewport and contains icons that are listed in a logical order for creating a final presentation.

Figure 1–6

- Hover the cursor over an icon to display its name and click it to open a panel that contains its related options, as shown for **Open File** in Figure 1–7.

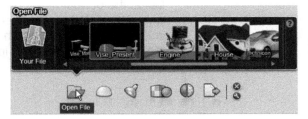

Figure 1–7

- At the top right corner of each panel, click ![help icon] to open the Help documentation about the panel that displays.

- To close the UI panel, click its icon again or click ![close icon] on the right side of the Task UI.

- Sometimes the Task UI interferes with the model in the viewport and you might want to temporarily remove it from the viewport. Click ![icon] on the right side of the Task UI and select **Show Task UI** to clear the option. To display the Task UI again, select **Options>Show Task UI** in the Menu Bar or press <Q>.

The Task UI panels are as follows:

Open File 📂

In an empty scene, only the Open File Task UI is available. You need to open a model to activate the other Task UI commands.

The Open File panel (shown in Figure 1–7), enables you to open the 3D CAD data file. Selecting the first swatch (**Your File**) opens the Open File dialog box in which you can select the file that you want to open. The rest of the Open File panel lists the recently opened files and the sample scenes included with the software. Recently opened files are listed on the left side followed by the list of sample scenes. If you open a sample scene, it is listed in the recently opened list and the images are duplicated. Use the slider bar at the bottom of the list to scroll through the list of recently opened and sample scenes and select an image to open its associated scene. Alternatively, you can use the **File>Open**, **File>Open Sample Scenes**, and **File>Open Recent** to open the required scenes.

The sample scenes included with the software are: Watch, Technicon, House, and Engine.

Lighting Environments and Background

The Lighting Environments & Background panel (shown in Figure 1–8), lists the different environments that are available for your scene. These are based on your model size. Use the slider bar at the bottom of the panel to move through the list. Select any of the listed environment images to apply them to your scene. The **Library** swatch on the right side of the panel opens the Environment interface in the viewport, which lists all of the available environments.

Figure 1–8

Adjust Lighting

*To modify the light and shadow properties of the current environment, you can also use the Directional Light and Shadows dialog box (**Appearance> Directional Light and Shadows**).*

The Adjust Lighting panel (shown in Figure 1–9) enables you to easily adjust and set the lighting and shadows included with the environment that is currently active in the scene.

Figure 1–9

Visual Styles

The Visual Styles panel (shown in Figure 1–10) enables you to change and set the visual appearance of the models in the scene. A list of preset visual styles is included with the software. Select the **Library** swatch in the Visual Styles panel to display a complete list of available visual styles in a menu form in the viewport. You can also open the Visual Styles panel by selecting **Appearance>Visual Styles Library** or pressing <V>. A short list of visual styles displays on the left side of the Visual Styles panel in the Task UI, based on the selected lighting environment. Use the slider bar to browse through the visual styles and click to assign the required visual style to the models in the scene.

Figure 1–10

Look ⬤

The Look panel (shown in Figure 1–11) enables you to display, create, and manage shots. It also enables you to open the Materials interface and then apply different materials and set various material properties. The left side of the Look panel contains the different shots of the scene, if they have already been created. Select a shot to open it. The **Shots** and **Materials** swatches on the right side of the panel open the Shots and Materials interfaces respectively.

Figure 1–11

Publish ⬛

The Publish panel (shown in Figure 1–12) enables you to publish the scene as an image or movie, to YouTube, and to the Web.

⬛ (Save) opens the Save Scene As dialog box and enables you to save your scene as an .A3S (Autodesk 3D scene) file or a compressed .ZIP file.

Figure 1–12

Hint: Hide the Main Menu toggle and Task UI at startup

You can use the User Settings dialog box to hide the Main

Menu toggle and Task UI at startup. Click ⬤ in the Task UI and select **User Settings** in the menu or select **File>Settings> User Settings** to open the User Settings dialog box. In the *Applications Settings* tab, in the *UI Settings* area, clear the **Show main menu toggle** and **Show Task UI at startup** options as shown in Figure 1–13. When you open the next session of the Autodesk Showcase software, the Main Menu

toggle (▼) and Task UI are not displayed. The Menu Bar

displays at the top of the viewport without ▼ . If you want to display the Task UI during the current session in which the Task UI is hidden at startup, select **Options>Show Task UI** or press \<Q>. If you want to display the Main Menu toggle or Task UI at the startup of the next session, select **File>Settings>User Settings** and select the required option in the User Settings dialog box.

UI Settings

☐ Show main menu toggle
☐ Show Task UI at startup

Locator Grips

Figure 1–13

3. Navigation Bar

The Navigation Bar is only available when a scene is open. It provides a quick way of accessing the most commonly used viewing and navigation tools (such as **Pan**, **Zoom**, **SteeringWheels**, **ViewCube**, and **Orbit**). The ViewCube is part of the Navigation tools and displays at the top of the Navigation Bar. The navigation tools that are available in the Navigation Bar are shown in Figure 1–14.

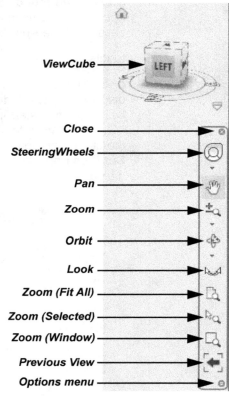

Figure 1–14

- The Navigation Bar displays in a very light gray until you hover the cursor over it.

- ⌐▾⌐ displayed below a tool indicates that it can be expanded and that additional options can be selected.

- Clicking **Close** at the top right corner of the Navigation Bar removes it from the viewport.

- To display the Navigation Bar in the viewport, select **View> Show Navigation Bar**.

- By default, the Navigation Bar is located at the top right side of the viewport. You can change its docking position to the top left, bottom right, or bottom left by expanding the Navigation Bar's **Options** menu (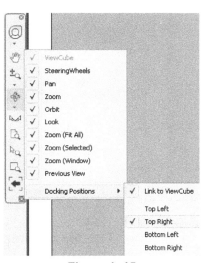), selecting **Docking Positions** and then selecting the required option, as shown in Figure 1–15. You can also control the display of tools in the Navigation Bar using the toggle option in the **Options** menu or by right-clicking on the tool and selecting **Remove from Navigation Bar**.

Figure 1–15

When you click any of the Navigation tool icons, the cursor displays the selected tool's image indicating that it is being used. If you use the tools in the Navigation Bar, you have to press <Esc> to exit the command.

The Navigation Bar contains the following tools:

(SteeringWheel)	Provides access to groups of commonly used navigation tools.
(Pan)	Enables you to move around to view the scene in the viewport by clicking and dragging the cursor in the direction in which you want to pan.
(Zoom)	Enables you to zoom in closer to the drawing or away from the drawing, displaying the results dynamically (in real time). ⬜▼ displays below it, indicating that additional options (**Zoom (Fit All)**, **Zoom (Selected)**, and **Zoom (Window)**) are available. These options are also available in the Navigation Bar.
(Zoom Fit All)	Enables you to fill the viewport with all of the objects in the scene. Alternatively, you can press <F> to display all of the objects in the Viewport window.

(Zoom Selected)	Enables you to fill the viewport with the selected object(s).
(Zoom Window)	Enables you to zoom into objects that are enclosed or passing through the selected window. Hold the left mouse button while you drag a window around the objects.
(Orbit)	Enables you to move the camera view around the set pivot point. Once in the command, the cursor displays as the **Orbit** icon and also displays a green pivot where it has been already set. ▼ displays below the icon, indicating that the additional **Orbit Constrained** option is available.
(Orbit Constrained)	Enables you to only orbit around the set pivot point in X-direction.
(Look)	Enables you look through the direction of a camera and move in that direction as you move the cursor while maintaining the camera in its original position and direction.
(Previous View)	Toggles between the two most recent views.

Center of Interest

By default, when you dynamically zoom and orbit in the viewport, you do so around the center of the model geometry (pivot point). When you press <Alt> a green pivot point displays in the model. If you want to zoom or orbit around a different point in the geometry, you can set the **Center of Interest** to the new point using any of the following methods:

- Hold <Ctrl>+<Alt> and click at the new location on the model geometry. This sets the pivot point at the selected point and moves this point to the center of the viewport.

- Hold <Alt> and click at the new location. This sets the pivot point at the selected point without relocating the model geometry.

If you want the pivot point to be positioned at the center of the model geometry, click ⌂ (Home) in the top left corner of the ViewCube (hover the cursor over the ViewCube to display ⌂). This returns the model to its original position and places the pivot point at the center.

Navigation using Keyboard Shortcuts

The easiest way to zoom, pan, and orbit is to use keyboard shortcuts or the mouse wheel without needing to start a command in the Navigation Bar. You can also exit the command by stopping the mouse and keyboard shortcuts.

Zoom	In the viewport, roll the mouse wheel away from you to zoom in and roll it toward you to zoom out. You can also hold <Alt> and the right mouse button and drag the cursor to dynamically zoom in and zoom out.
Pan	In the viewport, hold the mouse wheel and move the cursor to pan. You can also hold <Alt> and click and drag the mouse wheel to dynamically pan
Orbit	Hold <Alt> and click and drag the left mouse button to orbit around a pivot.

SteeringWheel

SteeringWheels provide access to groups of commonly used navigation tools. Depending on the selected wheel, you can access a small group of commands, such as **Zoom**, **Rewind**, **Orbit**, and **Pan**, or a group with many more options. The SteeringWheel displays at the cursor, enabling you to quickly select the navigation tools.

How To: Use the SteeringWheel

1. In the Navigation Bar, expand (Full Navigation Wheel) and select a SteeringWheel, as shown in Figure 1–16.

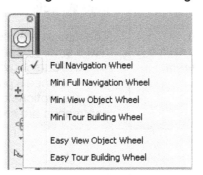

Figure 1–16

2. In the SteeringWheel, hover the cursor over the navigation command that you want to use, highlighting its wedge.
3. In the viewport, click and hold the mouse button to start the navigation command.
4. Move the cursor to change the view, as required.
5. Release the mouse button to end the navigation command.
6. Select another command or close the SteeringWheel.

- The SteeringWheel follows the cursor in the drawing window. Verify that the cursor is positioned correctly before launching a navigation command.

Full SteeringWheels

*Click the **X** icon in the SteeringWheel to close it.*

You can select from three different full wheels: Full Navigation, View Object, and Tour Building. The Full Navigation wheel includes all of the navigation tools, the View Object wheel contains **Center**, **Zoom**, **Rewind**, and **Orbit**, and the Tour Building wheel contains **Forward**, **Look**, **Rewind**, and **Up/Down**. The full wheels are shown in Figure 1–17.

Full Navigation

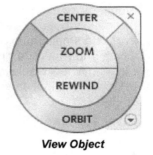
View Object

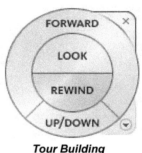
Tour Building

Figure 1–17

Mini Wheels

Right-click on the SteeringWheel to switch between the different types of wheels.

The mini wheels contain similar commands to the full wheels, but use a smaller icon with pie-shaped wedges. As the icon moves with the cursor (while you are in the **SteeringWheel** command), the mini wheels provide more screen space by eliminating the text descriptions on the wheel. The mini wheels and their commands are shown in Figure 1–18.

Zoom   Walk   Rewind   Up/Down   Pan   Look   Orbit   Center

Mini Full Navigation

Zoom   Rewind   Pan   Orbit   Walk   Rewind   Up/Down   Look

Mini View Object   *Mini Tour Building*

Figure 1–18

Rewind Command

Use the **Rewind** command to navigate to previously displayed views of the model, as shown in Figure 1–19.

Figure 1–19

How To: Use the Rewind Command

1. Start the **SteeringWheel** command.
2. Hover the cursor over the **Rewind** option.
3. Click and hold the mouse button to start the **Rewind** command. A series of thumbnails display.
4. Move the cursor over the thumbnails to navigate to the highlighted view. The model updates as you move over the thumbnails.
5. Release the mouse button to make the highlighted view active.

SteeringWheel Settings

The SteeringWheels Properties dialog box controls the appearance of the SteeringWheels. With a SteeringWheel active, right-click and select **Properties** to open the dialog box, as shown in Figure 1–20.

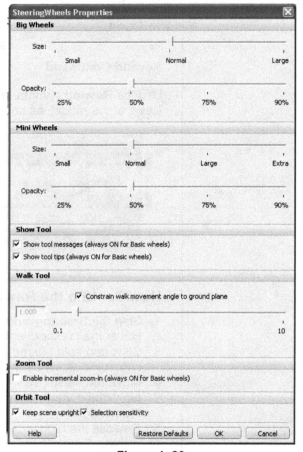

Figure 1–20

ViewCube

The ViewCube provides visual clues as to where you are in a 3D drawing and makes it easier to navigate to standard views, such as the top, front, right, corner, and directional views. In the ViewCube, hover the cursor over one of the faces, corners, or edges to highlight it and then select it to change the viewport to the selected view.

You can also click and drag the ViewCube to rotate the model. By default, the ViewCube is located at the top right corner of the viewport. It displays in light gray and ⌂ (Home) and ▽ are not displayed. Hover the cursor over the ViewCube to make it active and display the icons as shown in Figure 1–21. You can toggle the display of the ViewCube on by selecting **View>Show ViewCube**. If the ViewCube is not displayed in the viewport,

📦 (ViewCube) is added to the top of the Navigation Bar. Click

📦 (ViewCube), select **View>Show ViewCube**, or press <N> to display the ViewCube in the viewport.

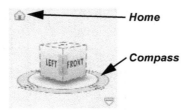

Figure 1–21

- Hover the cursor over any labeled orthographic view, such as FRONT, LEFT, etc., to highlight it and then click it to orient the model in the viewport to the selected view.

- Click on a corner or edge to orient the model to a perspective view.

- Click and drag the ViewCube to orbit around the geometry in the viewport. When using the **Orbit** command in the viewport, note that the ViewCube orbits to match the view in the viewport.

- Use the letters on the Compass (**N,S, E,** and **W**) to orbit to a face view in the cardinal direction.

- If you want to reorient the viewport and return to the Home view, click ⌂ (Home) or select **View>Go to Home View**. ⌂ (Home) displays when you hover the cursor over the ViewCube.

*To change the Home view and set it as the current view, click ▽ and select **Set Current View as Home** or right-click on the ViewCube and select **Set Current View as Home**.*

ViewCube Properties

ViewCube Properties control the display of the ViewCube, how it works when you are dragging or clicking, and several other settings. Click 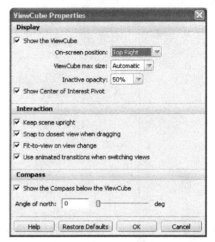 or right-click on the ViewCube and select **Properties** to open the ViewCube Properties dialog box, as shown in Figure 1–22.

Figure 1–22

Display Modes

Use <Tab> to toggle between the Standard and Presentation modes.

In the Autodesk Showcase software, use the following modes to display and work with the scenes:

- **Standard Mode**: The standard working mode for selecting, creating, and editing objects in the Viewport window.

- **Presentation Mode**: Intended for presenting a scene, such as selecting alternatives, playing shots, behaviors, and slides. In this mode, you cannot select and edit the objects in the viewport.

For an improved display, you can display the scene at the full extents of the monitor. This is done by hiding the Menu Bar and the viewport borders, including the Autodesk Showcase bar at the top and the Windows Task Bar at the bottom of the screen. To toggle the full screen display on or off, press <F9> or select **View>Full Screen**. Alternatively, a borderless window display style can also be used. This is similar to the full screen display in that the borders and Menu Bar are removed, but the software window is not maximized to the full extents of the monitor. To toggle the borderless window on or off, press <Ctrl>+<F9> or select **View>Borderless Window**.

1.4 Importing Models

The Autodesk Showcase software enables you to import 3D CAD geometry from various types of CAD design software. You can import a file or multiple files by selecting **File>Import> Import File(s)**. The Import File(s) dialog box opens, as shown in Figure 1–23.

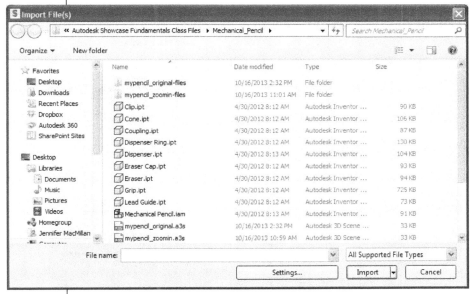

Figure 1–23

- You can either import a complete scene, which has already been compiled in the originating CAD software or import multiple files as separate files and combine them in the Autodesk Showcase software. To import multiple files, place them in a single folder, hold <Ctrl>, and select the required files.

- If you import an assembly file to which other files have been referenced (such as an .IAM file), the referenced files are imported with the assembly file.

- You can also import parts from other scenes into the currently open scene.

- The types of files that can be imported into the Autodesk Showcase software are listed in the All Supported File Types drop-down list in the Import File(s) dialog box, as shown in Figure 1–24.

Figure 1–24

- Once imported, the files are converted into the A3G format and loaded and made visible in the Autodesk Showcase viewport. This converted A3G file is not saved on import and you need to save it as a scene file. Once you have saved a scene file, you can import the geometry into other scene files without having to convert it again.

How To: Import a File

If a scene is already open, the objects from the selected file or files are merged into the current scene.

1. Select **File>Import>Import File(s)** to start the import.
2. In the Import File(s) dialog box, locate the required file folder.
3. Select a file from the list. You can also select several files to open at the same time in a single scene file. You can select multiple files by pressing <Ctrl> as you select the files.
4. Click **Import**.

The conversion process begins and 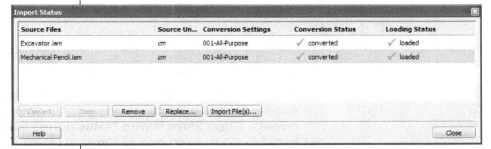 Converting displays in the bottom left corner of the viewport, indicating that it is working. Once the file has been completely converted, it is loaded into the viewport.

> **Hint: Import Models from Scene File**
>
> To import a scene file, select **File>Import>Import from Scene** to open the Import Files dialog box. This also opens with the **Import File(s)** command. The only difference is in the available list of *Files of Types*. The available files of types are only .A3S and .ZIP files.

Import Status

The Import Status dialog box (shown in Figure 1–25) tracks the conversion and loading process. You can review the list of imported files and modify them. Select **File>Import>Import Status Window** or press <I> to open the dialog box.

Figure 1–25

You can review the source file's units and conversion settings and whether the files were correctly converted and loaded. You can remove the selected file, replace it with another file, or import an additional file. Clicking **Replace...** and **Import File(s)...** opens the Import File(s) dialog box, enabling you to select a replacement file or additional file for importing.

If the imported geometry looks jagged and the quality is not good enough, you can set the *Conversion Settings* to a higher quality. Right-click on the *Conversion Settings* field for the selected geometry to display the available conversion settings, as shown in Figure 1–26. Generally for bigger models, you can leave the conversion settings as **All Purpose**. If small models need to be presented for marketing purposes, you might need to use **High Level of Detail (LOD)**. A High LOD uses a large number of polygons for a model and provides a much smoother appearance to the model. With a High LOD, the display might slow down.

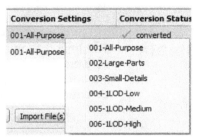

Figure 1–26

Hint: Display Import Status during Conversion Process

The Import Status dialog box can be open and interactively tracking the conversion and loading status during the import process. Select **Show Import Status during import** in the Import Settings dialog box, as shown in Figure 1–27.

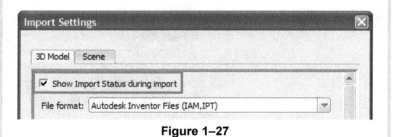

Figure 1–27

Import Settings

Import/Open
3D Model

↓

Import
Settings

↓

Convert to
A3G

↓

Save as .A3S

Before selecting a file for importing, review and adjust the import settings for the scene or geometry using the Import Settings dialog box, as shown in Figure 1–28. Select **File>Settings> Import Settings** to open the dialog box. Alternatively, if you are in the Import File(s)/Open File dialog box, click **Settings** to open the dialog box.

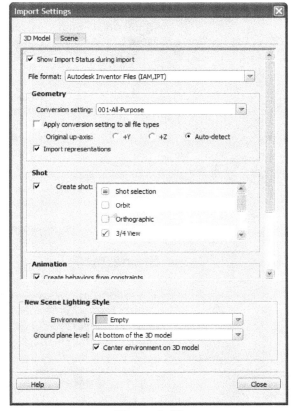

Figure 1–28

The Import Settings dialog box has two tabs: *3D Model* and *Scene.* They control the settings when you are importing a model or scene.

3D Model Tab

Show Import Status during import	Enables you to keep the Import Status dialog box open during the import and conversion process.
File format	Enables you to select a file format for importing. The areas and settings in the dialog box vary based on the selected file format.

Geometry area	Contains the list of the Level of Details required for the imported geometry. It also sets the **Original Up axis** settings to reorient the model while importing. • The **Import representations** option is only available for Autodesk Inventor files. It enables you to convert the positional representations in Autodesk Inventor files to shots and alternatives in the Autodesk Showcase software.
Shot: Create Shot area	Contains a list of available shots (**Orbit**, **Start to End**, **Track left**, etc.) that can automatically be created for the imported file. Enables you to create the shots for while importing a model. • The **Import AutoCAD views** option is only available for AutoCAD files. Enables you to import the AutoCAD views as shots. • The **Import all shots** option is only available for FBX files. Enables you to import all of the camera views available with the FBX file.
Animation area	Only available for Autodesk Inventor files and FBX files. Enables you to convert the constraints in the Autodesk Inventor files to behaviors in the Autodesk Showcase software. Automatically imports animations in the FBX file.

Scene Tab

The *Scene* tab (shown in Figure 1–29) contains settings that control the features that have to be imported while importing an already converted 3D Scene into another Autodesk Showcase scene. You can select the required features in the other scene.

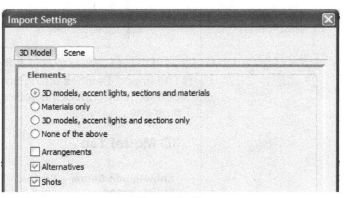

Figure 1–29

1.5 Open and Save Files

Opening the Files

The **Open** command enables you to open and edit an existing file as a new 3D scene. It closes the current file and opens the selected file as a new scene in one step. If your currently open scene contains unsaved changes, the software prompts you to save or discard the changes and opens the selected file as a new scene.

Files that have recently been opened can be reopened quickly using the (Open File) Task UI panel, which lists the recently opened files on the left side. Use the slider bar at the bottom of the list to scroll through the list and select an image to open its associated scene. Alternatively, you can use **File>Open Recent** to open the recently opened scenes.

How To: Open a Scene

1. Click (Your File) in (Open File) Task UI or select **File>Open**.
2. In the Open File dialog box locate the required file folder.
3. Select a file from the list.
4. Click **Open** or double-click on the file.

> **Hint: Opening and Importing Files**
>
> You can use the **Open** command or **Import** command to open different types of 3D CAD data files. With the **Import** command, you can import a single or multiple files into the currently open scene. The **Open** command closes the current scene and opens a single 3D file as a new scene.

Opening a New Scene

You can open a new empty scene by selecting **File>New**. This closes the current file and starts a new empty scene. If you have not saved the changes made to the previously open scene, the software prompts you to save or discard any changes.

The Autodesk Showcase software can only have one scene file open at a time, however multiple instances of the software can run simultaneously. To work on multiple scenes at the same time, open each scene in a separate instance of the Autodesk Showcase software.

Saving the Files

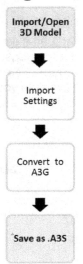

Import/Open
3D Model

⬇

Import
Settings

⬇

Convert to
A3G

⬇

Save as .A3S

Files are saved as scene files in the .A3S file format. The file contains information about all of the model files (.A3G), image files, and other associated files. You can save a scene file by selecting **File>Save** or **File>Save As**. The **Save As** command opens the Save Scene As dialog box in which you can browse to the folder in which you want to save the scene and enter a filename for the file. If you are using the **Save** command to save a scene file for the first time, it also opens the Save Scene As dialog box. Otherwise, the scene is automatically saved over the original saved file. You can save a file as a regular Autodesk 3D Scene File (.A3S) or as a Compressed Archive (.ZIP) file by selecting the required option in the Save as type drop-down list, as shown in Figure 1–30.

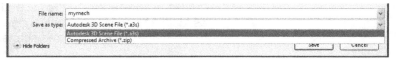

Figure 1–30

When you save a file, a new associated folder with the <filename>-files is created in the same folder as the scene file. This folder contains all of the associated files, such as shots, alternatives, etc. You can save the file as an .A3S file. However, if a file is associated to a large number of companion files, you need to use the .ZIP file format. In a .ZIP file, all of the referenced and companion files are saved with scene file and compressed together for easy maintenance and retrieval. You can open the .ZIP file in the Autodesk Showcase software as you would open an .A3S file.

Closing a File

You can close a file while leaving the Autodesk Showcase software open by selecting **File>Close**. The software prompts you to save any changes if you have not saved the scene. When you close the scene, the Navigation Bar and ViewCube also close, and only 📁 (Open File) remains active in the Task UI.

Practice 1a

Working with the Autodesk Showcase Interface

Practice Objectives

- Import a 3D data file and save the 3D scene.
- Navigate the user interface and open a new scene using the Task UI.

Estimated time for completion: 20 minutes

In this practice you will import an Autodesk Inventor file into the software. You will investigate the interface and navigate the scene using the navigation tools including the ViewCube. You will then save the scene as an .A3S file and open the file using the Task UI.

Task 1 - Open or import a file.

*If you launch the software for the first time, a Welcome screen displays. Click **Close**.*

1. If not already running, launch the Autodesk Showcase 2017 software.

2. Click ▼ at the top of the viewport window to display the Menu Bar.

*You can also use the **Import** command (**File> Import>Import File(s)**) if a new empty scene displays.*

3. In the Menu Bar, select **File>Open** or in the Task UI, click

   📁 (Open File) and click 🖼 (Your File) to open the Open File dialog box.

4. Browse to the practice files folder: *C:\Autodesk Showcase 2017 Fundamentals Practice Files*. Open the *Mechanical_ Pencil* folder.

5. Select **Mechanical Pencil.iam**. Do not open the file yet.

6. In the Open File dialog box, click **Settings...** to open the Import Settings dialog box.

---

7. In the *3D Model* tab, select **Show Import Status during import**, as shown in Figure 1–31.

8. In the *Geometry* area, verify that *Conversion setting* is set to **001-All Purpose**, as shown in Figure 1–31.

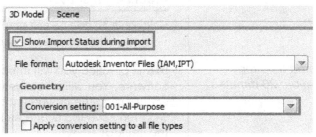

Figure 1–31

9. In the *New Scene Lighting Style* area, in the Environment drop-down list, select **Empty**, as shown in Figure 1–32. Click **Close**.

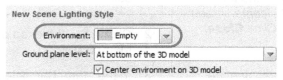

Figure 1–32

If a scene is already open, the software prompts you to save or discard the current scene before opening the selected file.

10. In the Open File dialog box, ensure that **Mechanical Pencil.iam** is still selected. Click **Open**.

11. In the Inventor Assembly Settings dialog box, click **Continue**.

Note that **Converting** displays in the bottom left corner of the viewport. The Import Status dialog box opens as well, displaying the *Conversion Status* as **converting**. Once the file has been completely loaded, the Import Status dialog box displays as shown in Figure 1–33. The model of the mechanical pencil is loaded in the viewport as a new scene.

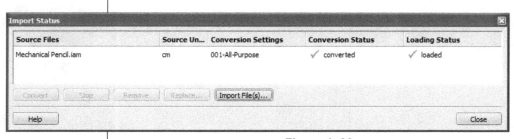

Figure 1–33

12. Click **Close** in the Import Status dialog box.

Task 2 - Using the Navigation Bar.

1. If you have a wheel mouse, scroll the wheel to zoom and press and drag it to pan.

2. In the Navigation Bar, click 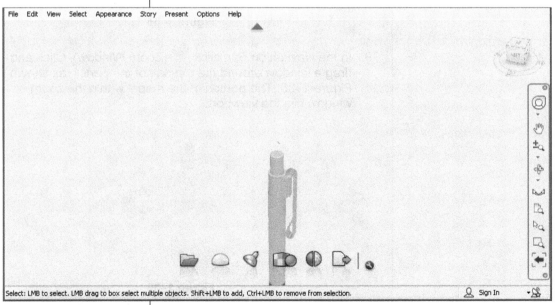 (Zoom Fit All) to refit the mechanical pencil so that it completely fills the viewport.

3. Hold <Alt> and note that the pivot point displays in the center of the mechanical pencil.

4. Hold <Alt> and click and drag the left mouse button to orbit around the pivot point in the pencil.

5. Hold <Alt> and click the left mouse button anywhere on the clip. This sets the pivot point at the selected point.

6. Hold <Ctrl>+<Alt> and click the left mouse button at the top point of the pencil (eraser). This sets the pivot point at the selected point and moves this point to the center of the viewport, as shown in Figure 1–34.

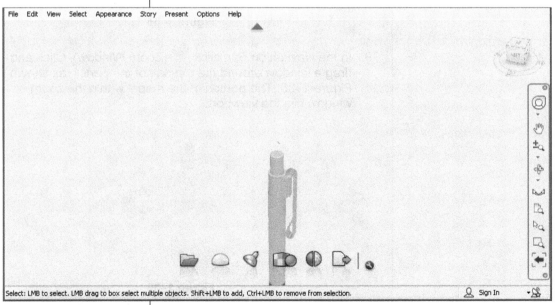

Figure 1–34

7. In the Navigation Bar, click 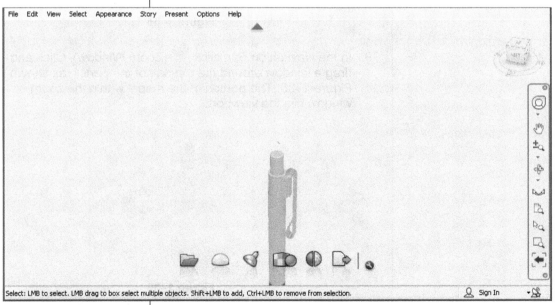 (Orbit). The cursor displays the **Orbit** icon. Click and drag the cursor to move the camera view around the pivot (around the top) toward the right so that the clip is not displayed, as it is hidden behind the pencil.

8. Click and hold again and move the cursor down so that the tip of the pencil is near the top of the viewport, as shown in Figure 1–35.

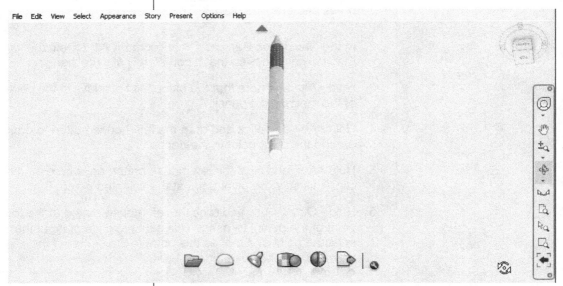

Figure 1–35

9. In the Navigation Bar, click 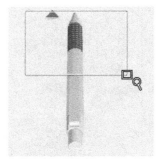 (Zoom Window). Click and drag a window around the top half of the pencil, as shown in Figure 1–36. The portion of the model within the zoom window fills the viewport.

Figure 1–36

Task 3 - Saving and Opening the Scene.

1. In the Menu Bar, select **File>Save** to open the Save Scene As dialog box. It opens because the file has not been saved before.

2. In the *File name* field, enter **mypencil_zoomin**. Note that by default the file is saved as an Autodesk 3D Scene File (*.A3S) as shown in Figure 1–37. Click **Save**.

Figure 1–37

You can also press <Ctrl>+<W> to close the current scene.

3. In the Menu Bar, select **File>Close** to close the current scene and to display an empty scene.

4. In the Task UI, click (Open File) and click (Your File) to open the Open File dialog box. Browse to the *Mechanical_Pencil* folder of your practice files folder, if it is not already open. Note that along with the saved **mypencil_zoomin.a3s** file, a *mypencil_zoomin-files* folder has been created automatically, as shown in Figure 1–38.

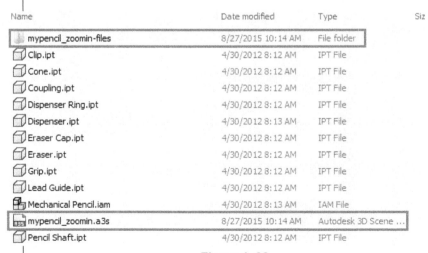

Figure 1–38

5. Select **mypencil_zoomin.a3s** and click **Open**. The file opens in the viewport similar to that shown in Figure 1–39.

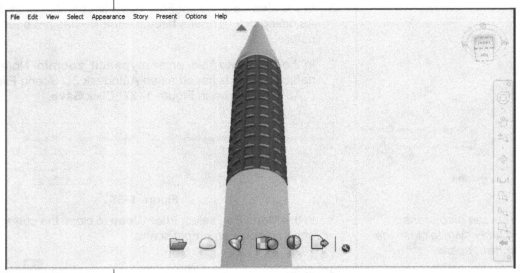

Figure 1–39

6. In the ViewCube, at the top right corner of the viewport, hover the cursor over the **TOP** label to highlight it and then click it to orient the model in the viewport to the top view. The model will display similar to that shown in Figure 1–40.

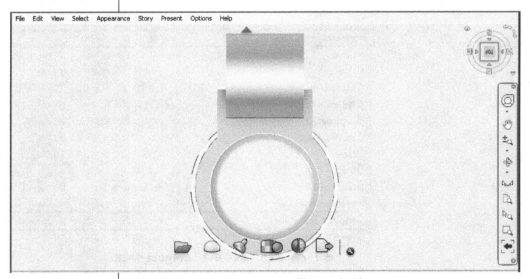

Figure 1–40

7. In the ViewCube, hover the cursor over the left edge to highlight it, as shown in Figure 1–41. Click it to orient the 3D model to the top right perspective view.

Figure 1–41

8. In the Navigation Bar, click 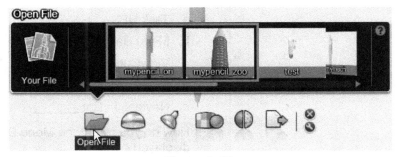 (Previous View) to go back to the Top view of the model.

9. Use other orientation views, including the corner and edge positions in the ViewCube.

10. When finished, hover the cursor over the ViewCube and click

    (Home) to orient the pencil to the original import position.

11. In the Menu Bar, select **File>Save As** to open the Save Scene As dialog box and save the scene as **mypencil_original.a3s**.

12. In the Task UI, click (Open File). Note that both files (**mypencil_zoomin** and **mypencil_original**) are listed in the recent files list, as shown in Figure 1–42.

Figure 1–42

13. Select **File>Close to** close the file. Note that the Navigation Bar and ViewCube also close, and only (Open File) remains active in the Task UI.

The software prompts you to save any changes, if you have not saved the scene.

Chapter Review Questions

1. Match the interface components listed below to the numbers shown in Figure 1–43.

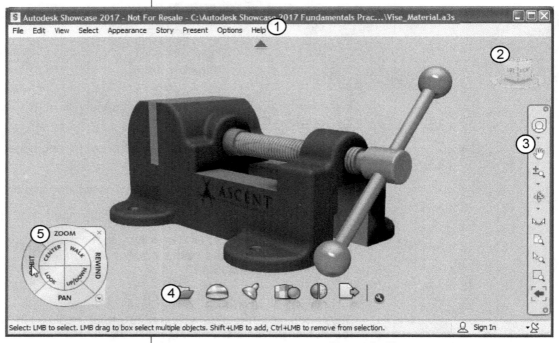

Figure 1–43

   a. Task UI _____
   b. Menu Bar _____
   c. ViewCube _____
   d. SteeringWheel _____
   e. Navigation Bar _____

2. How do you return the Menu Bar to the interface if it is not displayed?

   a.
   b.
   c.
   d.

3. The **Open File** tools in the Task UI have a scroll bar that can be used to open files. Which files are listed in this scroll list? (Select all that apply.)

   a. Previously viewed files.

   b. All of the files in the current active directory.

   c. Sample files.

4. Which of the following procedures best describes how to change the Pivot Point?

   a. Hold <Alt> and select a new point.

   b. Hold <Alt> and right-click on a new point.

   c. Hold <Ctrl> and select a new point.

   d. Hold <Ctrl> and right-click on a new point.

5. Which of the following images represents the Mini Full Navigation Wheel?

   a.

   b.

   c. (Pan)

   d. (Orbit)

6. Which of the following ViewCube images sets an isometric view?

a.

b.

c.

d.

7. Which of the following can be done in the Import Status dialog box? (Select all that apply.)

a. Change the conversion setting to **LOD-High**.

b. Prevent the Import Status dialog box from opening on the next import.

c. Import additional files.

d. Replace files.

8. When using the **Open** command to open 3D CAD files in the Autodesk Showcase software, you can only open a single file at one time.

a. True

b. False

Command Summary

Interface Component	Access Location
Adjust Lighting	• **Task UI:**
Lighting Environments and Backgrounds	• **Task UI:** • **Menu Bar:** Appearance>Lighting Environment Library • **Shortcut Key:** <E>
Look (Manage Shots and Materials)	• **Task UI:** • **Menu Bar:** Story>Camera Shots or Appearance>Material Library • **Shortcut Key:** <T> or <M>
Open File	• **Task UI:** • **Menu Bar:** File>Open
Publish	• **Task UI:** • **Menu Bar:** File>Publish (*Image, Movie, YouTube, or Web Presentation*)
Visual Styles	• **Task UI:** • **Menu Bar:** Appearance>Visual Style Library • **Shortcut Key:** Press <V>

Adjusting the Models

In this chapter, you learn how to select objects, organize the parts in a scene, transform and duplicate objects, and adjust the geometry by fixing the normals. You also learn how to use the different Visual Styles and understand the available rendering modes.

Learning Objectives in this Chapter

- Select objects in the viewport using the various selection methods and selection display styles.
- View object hierarchy, select and edit objects using the Organizer.
- Check and correct the surface normals of your imported geometry.
- Edit and extract patches in an object.
- Modify objects using the transform tools and revert the objects back to their original transforms.
- Delete and restore objects using Delete and Undo commands.
- Create copy or multiple copies of objects using the various Duplicate options.
- Apply the various visual styles.
- Control the settings of Hardware rendering and Ray Tracing rendering methods.

Autodesk Showcase Workflow

Figure 2–1 shows the overall suggested workflow for the Autodesk® Showcase® software. The horizontal line at the top represents the high-level workflow and each of their sub-steps are detailed vertically below them. The highlighted column represents the content discussed in the current chapter.

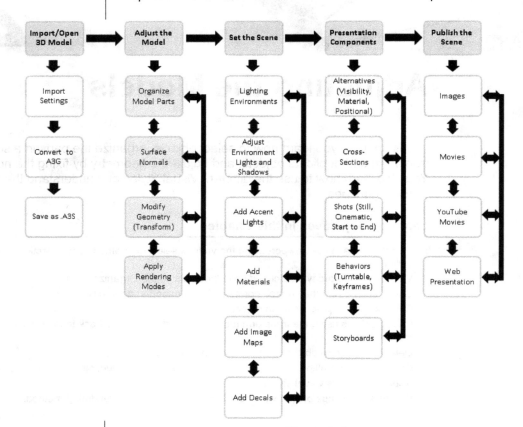

Figure 2–1

2.1 Selecting Objects

Once the model is available in the viewport, you need to select objects or geometry to modify the features and change the settings of the geometry. The Autodesk Showcase software enables you to select geometry using a variety of methods. The easiest method is to click on the required geometry to select it. Once selected, it is highlighted with the selected display style to enable you to identify it easily, as shown in Figure 2–2.

Figure 2–2

Selection Display Styles

You can control how you want the selected geometry to be displayed in the viewport. By default, a blue animated grid (it is moving) highlights the selected geometry. You can select any of the following display styles:

- Animated Grid

- White Wireframe

- Black Wireframe

- Blue Wireframe

The selected Selection Display Style is saved with the software session. Therefore, when you open a new session of the software, it uses the selection style from the last session.

These can be set by selecting **Options>Selection Display Style** and then selecting the required option, as shown on the right in Figure 2–3. You can also select the selection display style in the Selection Style drop-down list (as shown on the left in Figure 2–3), in the User Settings dialog box. You can open this dialog box by selecting **File>Settings>User Settings**.

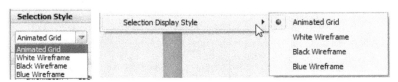

Figure 2–3

Selection Methods

If you cannot select objects in the scene, press <Tab> to exit the Presentation mode.

The different methods that can be used for selecting objects in the viewport are as follows:

Using the Mouse

- Click on the geometry that you want to select.

- Hold <Shift> and click additional parts in the model to select multiple geometry.

- Hold <Ctrl> to remove geometry from the selection.

- Press <Esc> or click anywhere in empty space to exit the selection.

The Autodesk Showcase software prompts you about the mouse selection options at the bottom of the viewport screen, as shown in Figure 2–4.

Select: LMB to select. LMB drag to box select multiple objects. Shift+LMB to add, Ctrl+LMB to remove from selection.

Figure 2–4

Using the Menu

The **Select** menu in the Menu Bar has various options (as shown in Figure 2–5), that enable you to make the appropriate selection quickly and easily.

Figure 2–5

- **Select All:** Selects all of the available geometry and lights in the scene. It also selects the hidden geometry. If there is some hidden geometry and you select this option, a warning message displays in the viewport, as shown in Figure 2–6. You can also press <Ctrl>+<A> to use the **Select All** option.

Figure 2–6

- **Select All Visible:** Selects all of the visible geometry and lights. Press <Ctrl>+<K>.

- **Deselect All:** Clears all of the selected geometry and lights. Press <Ctrl>+<Shift>+<A>.

- **Deselect Hidden:** Only clears the selected hidden geometry. The visible geometry and light remain selected. Press <Ctrl>+<Shift>+<K>.

Using the Selection Window

Click and hold anywhere in empty space near the objects that you want to select. Drag toward the opposite corner to create a window around the objects that you want to select. Leave the cursor to make the selection. All of the objects that are present inside the window are selected, including objects that are underneath and objects that are touching the selection window. You can then use <Shift> and <Ctrl> to add or clear geometry from the selection.

Using the Shortcut Menu

Right-click on an object in the viewport to display its specific shortcut menu, as shown in Figure 2–7. The menu has options that enable you to make selections specific to that object.

Hover the cursor over an option to highlight the associated geometry in the viewport.

Select:
All objects with this material
All objects with this material type
Sleeve:1_BODY
Sleeve:1
Mechanical Pencil.iam
Files ▶
Layers ▶
Objects behind ▶
Edit:
Material Properties…
In Scene Material Properties…

Figure 2–7

- The first section in the menu contains options for selecting geometry that have the same material or material type as the menu object.

- The next section of the menu displays a list of object names. You can select the object itself, the parent object, or the object to which it belongs.

- In the next section you can select objects in the form of files and layers. Selecting **Files** and **Layers** in the menu opens a submenu that lists the objects that belong to those two folders.

- Selecting **Objects behind** opens a submenu listing the objects that are behind the object, as shown in Figure 2–8. You can then select the required objects from the list.

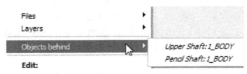

Figure 2–8

Using the Organizer

If geometry is created using many separate and small parts, selecting individual parts in the viewport can be difficult. You can use the Organizer dialog box to select the individual parts.

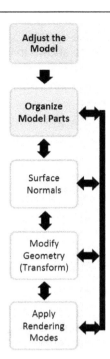

2.2 Organizer Dialog Box

The Organizer dialog box lists all of the parts and geometry that are imported into the Autodesk Showcase scene in the form of a tree structure, as shown in Figure 2–9. The Organizer is a modeless dialog box and remains open regardless of the task that you are performing. It can be toggled open or closed by selecting **Edit>Organizer** or pressing <O>.

Figure 2–9

The organizer can be used to perform the following actions:

- **View original hierarchy:** Click ⊕ next to a part to expand its part list and click ⊖ to collapse it.

- **Select objects:** Select an object or multiple objects (holding <Ctrl> or <Shift>) in the organizer (they display in orange). These objects are selected in the viewport.

- **Display visibility:** Select a part and click 👁 to hide the object in the viewport. Select a hidden part and click ⬭ to make it visible in the viewport. Note that the hidden objects are listed in italics in the Organizer. You can also use 👁 / 👁 in the Organizer toolbar to **Hide/Show** the parts.

You can also right-click on an object in the Organizer to access all of the Organizer tools.

- **Transform objects:** Select a part and double-click on 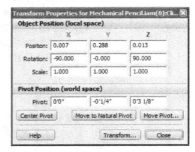 to open the Transform Properties dialog box, as shown in Figure 2–10.

Figure 2–10

If an object has been transformed from its original position or

rotation, 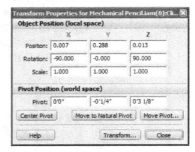 displays next to the transformed object.

- **Object properties:** You can change the size of the object by right-clicking on it and selecting **Object Properties** (as shown in Figure 2–11) to open the Object Properties dialog box, as shown in Figure 2–12.

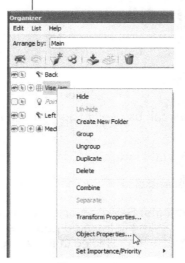

Figure 2–11

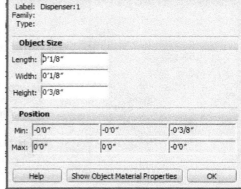

Figure 2–12

- **Reorganize objects:** Click (Create new folder) in the toolbar to open a new folder and then drag-and-drop the objects into this new folder.

- **Grouping objects:** In the Organizer, select the objects and click 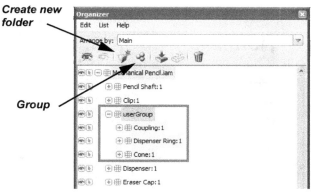 (Group). Grouping enables multiple objects to be treated as a single unit, but you can control each object separately as well. The selected objects are grouped in a newly created folder called *userGroup*, as shown in Figure 2–13. You can double-click on *userGroup* and rename the group as required.

Create new folder

Group

Figure 2–13

Use Combine objects to improve the speed of the rendering process when you are interactively presenting a scene.

- **Combine objects:** Select a group and click 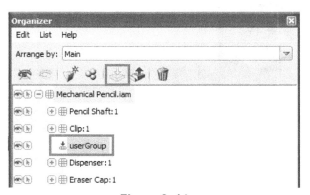 (Combine). The group is combined and the individual objects are not visible anymore, as shown in Figure 2–14.

Figure 2–14

- **Separate objects:** Select a combined group and click (Separate) to list the individual objects.

- **Delete objects:** Select a part and click 🗑 (Delete) in the toolbar. You can select **Edit>Undo** in the Main Menu to undo the delete.

2.3 Adjust the Imported Models

After you import geometry into the Autodesk Showcase software, there might be discrepancies in the geometry or in the placement of the geometry. It is recommended that you resolve those issues before you modify the scene and manipulate the design for presentation.

Surface Normals

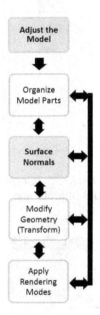

The surface of an object consists of polygonal faces and the orientation of these faces depends on the direction of the surface normals. Normals are imaginary vectors that are located perpendicular to one side of each face. The normals should face toward the viewer for the applied materials to display as required. The imported geometry automatically has its surface normal direction pointing to the outside, but sometimes it needs to be corrected.

Checking and Correcting Surface Normals

Before applying materials and editing the geometry, verify that all of the normals are facing outside and correct the surfaces that have reversed normals.

*   You can press <F7> to set the model geometry shading to display normals. The normals that are facing outward display in blue and the faces with normals facing inward display in yellow, as shown in Figure 2–15.

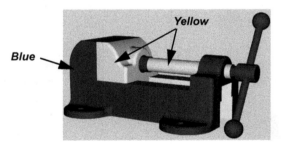

Figure 2–15

*   In the Show Normal mode, you cannot assign or edit materials.

*You have to select faces for <F8> and **Edit> Reverse Normals** to be active.*

*   Select the yellow geometry in the model and press <F8> or select **Edit>Reverse Normals**. The yellow faces display in blue indicating that the faces are oriented correctly (facing outward).

Press <V> again to remove the Visual Styles interface from the viewport.

- To exit Show Normal mode, press <Esc> or press <V> to display the Visual Styles interface and select a different visual style. Alternatively, in the Task UI, click 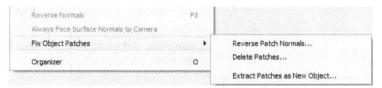 (Visual Style) and then select a visual style. Note that **Normals** is a visual style in the *Diagnostics* category, but it can only be applied outside the Visual Styles interface.

Fix Object Patches

Patches are specific polygons that are part of a single object and cannot be selected individually. When you want to place an image of a specific part of a single object or when some polygons of a bigger object are irregular and their surface normals are not fixed with the original object, you might want to edit those surfaces separately. To do so you need to extract them as new objects. Select **Edit>Fix Object Patches** to access the options that are available for patches, as shown in Figure 2–16.

Reverse Normals	F8
Always Face Surface Normals to Camera	
Fix Object Patches	▶	Reverse Patch Normals...
Organizer	O	Delete Patches...
		Extract Patches as New Object...

Figure 2–16

Reverse Patch Normals

If an object containing patches whose normals are facing the wrong direction (as shown in Figure 2–17), use the **Reverse Patch Normals** option.

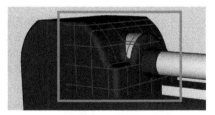

Figure 2–17

How To: Reverse Patch Normals

1. Select the part with the yellow patch.
2. Select **Edit>Fix Object Patches>Reverse Patch Normals** to open the Fix Object Patches dialog box.
3. In the Fix Object Patches dialog box, select **Reverses its normals** as shown in Figure 2–18.

---

4. In the viewport, select the yellow patch. It displays in blue and a checkmark displays in *Reverse* column for the patch number in the dialog box, as shown in Figure 2–18. Select other yellow patches, as required.

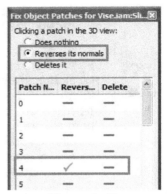

Figure 2–18

Use the **Deletes it** option to clear any previously reversed patches. Alternatively, you can select **Edit>Fix Object Patches>Delete Patches**.

Extract Patches

If an object has been modeled as a single object, you might want to manipulate or edit a portion of it or break it into separate objects by extracting sections. You can extract sub-objects from an object and create a completely separate object.

How To: Extract Patches

1. Select **Edit>Fix Object Patches>Extract Patches as New Object**. The Extract Patches as New Object dialog box opens, as shown in Figure 2–19. All of the objects in the scene display in light purple, indicating that it is in Extraction mode.

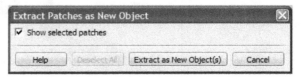

Figure 2–19

2. In the viewport, select the patches for extraction. You can select one or multiple objects. The selected patches display in a gray shade.
3. Click **Extract as New Object(s)**.

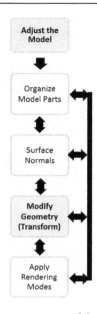

Adjust the Model

Organize Model Parts

Surface Normals

Modify Geometry (Transform)

Apply Rendering Modes

2.4 Transforming Geometry

Transforms are used to move, rotate, or scale objects to fit with other objects in the scene. You might want to relocate objects with respect to other objects in the scene or change the size or orientation of an object to display a different side of the object in the scene. You can use the **Transform** tools to make the changes. To transfer objects, you can use either of the following methods:

- Use the transform handles to graphically transform objects in the viewport.

- Enter the exact values to transform an object in all of the axes using the Transform dialog box.

- Use the Transform Properties dialog box to enter the exact values with respect to the current position of the object.

Using Transform Handles

You can display the transform handles when you select an object in the viewport. By default, the transform handles are not displayed. To display the transform handles while selecting an object (as shown in Figure 2–20), press <H> or select **Edit> Show Transform Handles**. The transform handles display at the pivot point of the selected object, which is the spatial center of that object, as shown for the left and front views of the object in Figure 2–20. The transformations are applied relative to the pivot point.

Transform Handles

Perspective view

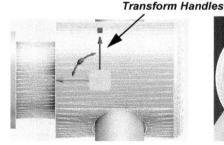

Left view

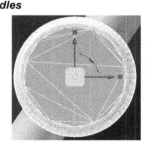

Front view

Figure 2–20

If multiple objects are selected, the transform handles display at the spatial center of all of the selected objects, as shown in Figure 2–21.

Figure 2–21

Click and drag any direction arrow, square box, curved double-sided arrow, center square plate, or center square box to apply the associated transform. The different handles are as follows:

	Click and drag any of the three arrows to move the object in the specific X-, Y-, or Z-axis.
	Click and drag any of the three square boxes to scale the object in the specific X-, Y-, or Z-axis.
	Click and drag any of the three curved double-sided arrows to rotate the object in the specific X-, Y-, or Z-axis.
	Click and drag the square plane at the center of the handles to move the object in any free direction.
	Click and drag the square box at the center of the square plane to scale the objects equally in all directions.
	Press <Insert>. The square box in the center of the position transform plane displays as a green dot, which is the pivot point. Click and drag any move transform handle to move the pivot of the object.

How To: Use the Transform Handles to Apply Transformations

1. In the viewport, select an object and press <H> if the transform handles are not displayed.
2. Click and drag any of the arrows to dynamically reposition the object in a specific direction, as shown for repositioning in the X-axis in Figure 2–22.

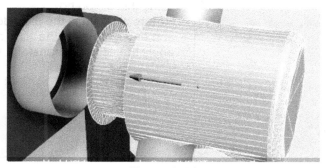

Figure 2–22

3. Similarly, you can click and drag other icon handles to rotate and scale the object.

Hint: Using the Heads-up Display for Transformations

You can select any transform handle to open its heads-up display and enter exact values for that transformation, as shown in Figure 2–23.

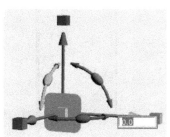

Figure 2–23

Using the Transform Dialog Box

You can transform objects (**Move** and **Rotate**) in all of the axes at the same time by entering the exact values in the Transform dialog box, as shown in Figure 2–24. You can open this dialog box by clicking  (Outer Plane) in the transform handles. You can also open this dialog box by clicking **Transform** in the Transform Properties dialog box (**Edit>Transform>Transform Properties**). You can only apply the Move and Rotate transform using this dialog box. Select either **Translate relative** (Move) or **Rotate relative** in the drop-down list (as shown in Figure 2–24), and enter values in the X, Y, and Z edit boxes. Click **Apply** to apply the selected transform to the selected object.

Figure 2–24

Using Transform Properties

If you want to transform objects with respect to their original values when imported, select an object in the viewport, and select **Edit>Transform>Transform Properties**, to open the Transform Properties dialog box, as shown in Figure 2–25.

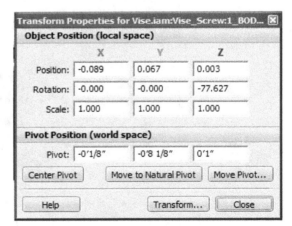

Figure 2–25

In the *Object Position* area, you can enter values for the Position, Rotation, and Scale transforms to apply the transforms in the X-, Y-, and Z-axes. The values entered transform the geometry with respect to original values at the time of import. Note that some values are already displayed in the edit boxes. They indicate the original values of the selected object at the time of import. If you select multiple entries and open the dialog box, the values displayed are from the object that is highest in the hierarchy. The object hierarchy is available in the Organizer dialog box.

In the *Pivot Position* area, you can set the pivot position of the object in world space.

Repeat and Revert Transforms

An important transform feature is that the software enables you to repeat any transform by copying it from the object on which it has been applied and then pasting it on the object on which you want it to repeat. The **Copy Transform** and **Paste Transform** can be accessed from **Edit>Transform**, as shown in Figure 2–26.

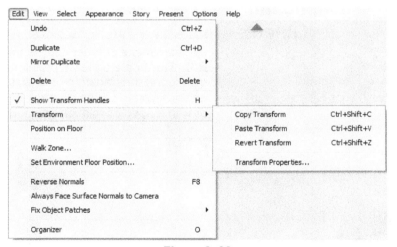

Figure 2–26

You can return the object to its original import position and size by selecting **Edit>Transform>Revert Transform**. Select the complete model (all of the parts) using <Ctrl>+<A> or by selecting the complete object list in the Organizer and selecting **Revert Transform**.

2.5 Duplicating and Deleting Objects

You can undo, delete, and make copies of objects using the **Edit** menu as shown in Figure 2–27.

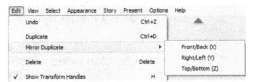

Figure 2–27

Delete and Undo

To delete an object from the scene, select it and select **Edit> Delete**. You can also press <Delete> after selecting an object. To restore the object, select **Edit>Undo** or press <Ctrl>+<Z>.

Duplicating Objects

Select an object that you want to copy, and select **Edit> Duplicate**. The object is copied over the original object. Using a transform handle, you can move or rotate the copied object. You can then make another copy of the duplicated object by selecting **Edit>Duplicate** again or pressing <Ctrl>+<D>. This copies the object and the transform that was used on the first copy. This enables you to create an array of objects at a specified distance or with a specific rotation as shown in Figure 2–28.

Figure 2–28

You can also use **Edit>Mirror Duplicate** and select an option for the mirroring criteria to create duplicated geometry. The mirrored copy of the selected object is created with respect to the selected axis.

2.6 Visual Styles

Visual styles provide you with a variety of ways to view objects in the scene. A standard set of styles is available that enable you to view your scenes so that they display as they would in the final presentation without modifying the material properties. The visual styles are accessed in the Visual Styles interface, as shown in Figure 2–29.

- To open the Visual Styles interface, select **Appearance> Visual Styles Library** or press <V>. Alternatively, you can

  click  in the Visual Styles Task UI.

- The available visual styles display as swatches and categorized under **Realistic**, **Abstract**, and **Diagnostics**. Select a swatch to apply the visual style to the objects in the scene. It displays a set of standard visual properties, such as shadows, ray tracing, non-photorealistic effects, etc.

- The visual style that is currently being used in the scene is surrounded by a blue border with arrows.

*Press <V> again or click the **X** icon to remove the Visual Styles interface from the viewport.*

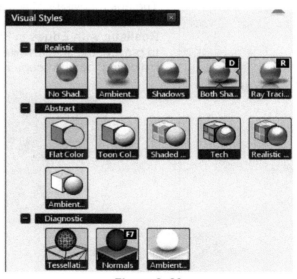

Figure 2–29

The Both Shadows and Ambient Shadows visual style and the Ray Tracing style can be applied outside the Visual Style interface by pressing <D> and <R> respectively.

Realistic Visual Styles

The realistic visual styles enable you to display the scenes with high-quality photorealistic shading, which is similar to a realistic look of the scene. Depending on the selected style, the shadows are toggled on or off, and the hardware rendering or ray-tracing are enabled. Some of the realistic visual styles are shown in Figure 2–30.

No Shadows   *Both Shadows & Ambient Shadows*   *Ray Tracing*

Figure 2–30

Abstract Visual Styles

The abstract visual styles enable you to display the scenes in a non-photorealistic display, as shown for **Toon Color** and **Realistic with Edges** in Figure 2–31. These styles enable you to present the scene while you are still in the design phase, indicating that the scene is not complete.

Toon Color   *Realistic with Edges*

Figure 2–31

Diagnostic Visual Styles

*The **Normals** visual style can be displayed outside the Visual Style interface by pressing <F7>.*

As the name indicates, the diagnostic visual styles enable you to display your scenes with a style that helps you to troubleshoot the geometry, normals, and ambient shadows. The Tessallation visual style is shown in Figure 2–32.

Tessallation
Figure 2–32

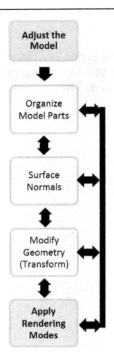

2.7 Rendering Modes

All of the scenes in the Autodesk Showcase software are rendered in real time. Two rendering methods are used in the software: *Hardware rendering* and *Interactive Ray Tracing*. Depending on the selected visual style, the rendering method is enabled.

Hardware Rendering

This is the default rendering for displaying the scenes. It uses the GPU (Graphics Processing Unit) to render calculations and the response time is fast. Therefore, it is easier to transform geometry, modify materials and cameras, and output images. You can control the hardware rendering quality in the Performance and Quality dialog box (*Hardware Rendering* tab), as shown in Figure 2–33. Select **File>Settings>Performance and Quality** to open the dialog box.

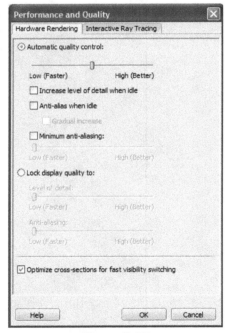

Figure 2–33

- Use the **Automatic quality control** slider to increase or decrease the visual quality of the scene. By default, it is set at the middle. The software automatically adjusts the frame rate (speed) of the scene based on the position of the slider. The higher the quality, the lesser the frame rate speed.

- Select **Increase level of detail when idle** to have the highest level of detail when the scene is idle.

- Antialiasing is the process of smoothing jagged diagonal lines and curves that display in visuals. In the example shown on the left in Figure 2–34, the image was rendered with antialiasing. The image shown on the right was rendered without antialiasing. If diagonals and curves seem to be too *edgy* you can experiment with the available antialiasing options. Enabling antialiasing improves the quality but the slows down the speed.

Figure 2–34

- The **Lock display quality to** option enables you to set the LOD and Antialiasing options for specific objects in the scene and to set the rest of the objects that are not the focus of the presentation to **Automatic quality control**. This improves the performance of the scene display.

Ray Tracing

Ray tracing is a rendering method that is used to calculate accurate reflections, refractions, and shadows. It adds realistic shadows and reflections to the scene and produces very high-quality visualizations. This method uses the CPU (Central Processing Unit) for calculations, which can affect the speed and performance of the software. When the Ray Tracing visual style is selected for the scene, ray tracing is enabled in the Ray Tracing Status panel (as shown in Figure 2–35), which displays in the lower right corner of the viewport.

Only the Ray Tracing visual style renders the scene using the Ray Tracing rendering method.

Figure 2–35

- It displays the progress of the rendering, including the time elapsed (hours:minutes:seconds) and the render levels completed up to this time.

- Click **Save** to open the Save Image As dialog box. You can save the current image in the viewport as a .JPG or .TIFF file. It also automatically generates an .XML file, which contains all of the ray tracing settings.

- Click **Settings** to open the Performance and Quality dialog box. In the *Interactive Ray Tracing* tab, you can control the ray tracing quality, as shown in Figure 2–36. You can also set the Ray Tracing settings before you start rendering a scene, by selecting **File>Settings>Performance and Quality>** *Interactive Ray Tracing* tab.

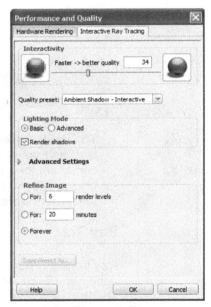

Figure 2–36

Practice 2a

Organizing and Transforming the Objects

Practice Objectives

Estimated time for completion: 30 minutes

- Select objects and duplicate and reposition a part.
- Organize and group the parts.

In this practice you will use the various selection methods to select the objects. You will duplicate a part and position it at the required location using the various Transform methods. You will also reorganize some parts and group them separately using the Organizer.

Task 1 - Selecting parts.

1. Click (Your File) in the (Open File) Task UI or select **File>Open**.

2. In the Open File dialog box, in your practice files folder, open the *Vise_Organize* folder, select **Vise-Initial.a3s**, and click **Open**. A 3D model of the vise opens in the viewport, as shown in Figure 2–37. Note that the handle only has a ball on one side.

Figure 2–37

*The selection display style depends on the last selected style. Select **Options> Selection Display Style** to change the display style.*

3. Click to select any part of the object. Note that a blue animated grid displays on the part indicating that it has been selected (if **Animated Grid** was the last selected style).

4. Select the handle ball. Right-click on it to display the selection menu as shown in Figure 2–38. Note that the name of the ball (**Handle_Ball:2**) is listed with its related objects (**Screw_Sub:1** and **Vise.iam**).

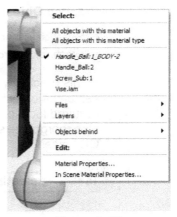

Figure 2–38

5. Hover the cursor over **Screw_Sub:1** to highlight the associated parts in the viewport. Hover the cursor over **Vise.iam** and note that all of the parts are highlighted because **Vise.iam** is at the top of the hierarchy. Press <Esc>.

*You can also select **Edit>Organizer** to open the Organizer.*

6. With the ball still selected, press <O> to open the Organizer and note that only **Vise.iam** is displayed and highlighted. This indicates that a part(s) in its hierarchy list has been selected.

7. In the Organizer, click ⊕ next to **Vise.iam** to expand its part list. Note that **Screw_Sub:1** is highlighted. Click ⊕ next to **Screw_Sub:1** to display its parts list and note that **Handle_Ball:2** is highlighted as shown in Figure 2–39.

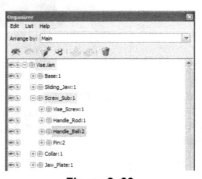

Figure 2–39

8. In the viewport, select other parts and note that the relevant parts in the Organizer list are highlighted. Keep the Organizer open.

Task 2 - Transforming the objects.

You can also press <Ctrl>+<D> to duplicate objects.

1. Verify that the **Handle_Ball:2** is still selected (if not, select it first), in the Menu Bar, select **Edit>Duplicate**. The part is duplicated on top of the original one. It is also displayed in the Organizer, with the second **Handle_Ball:2** listed under **Screw_Sub:1**.

2. In the Organizer, double-click on the second **Handle_Ball:2** and change its name to **Handle_Ball:1**, as shown in Figure 2–40. Press <Enter>. In the viewport, click in empty space to clear the selection.

Figure 2–40

3. In the ViewCube, select **FRONT** (as shown in Figure 2–41), to change the display orientation to the Front view.

Figure 2–41

4. In the Organizer, select **Handle_Ball:1** to select the duplicated ball.

*You can also use the **Edit>Show Transform Handles** to toggle the handles on or off.*

5. Right-click in the viewport to activate it. Press <H> to toggle on the Transform Handles, if they are not already displayed.

6. Click [ ] (Transform Plane) to open the Transform dialog box. Note that you must select around the exterior of this button (not the inner box) to activate the dialog box. (Clicking on the inner box opens a heads-up entry field for the active transform.)

The units displayed in the Transform dialog box depend on the units specified in the User Settings dialog box, not on the model units.

7. Verify that **Transform relative** is selected and set X to **0'2"** (**5 cm**) and Z to **0'4"** (**10 cm**). Click **Apply** as shown in Figure 2–42. The ball moves closer to the opposite side of **Handle_Rod:1**. Close the Transform dialog box.

Figure 2–42

- In the Organizer, note that  displays next to **Handle_Ball:1** (as shown in Figure 2–43), indicating that it has been modified.

Figure 2–43

8. In the Navigation Bar, click ⌕ (Zoom Window). Click and drag a window around **Handle_Ball:1** and the top portion of **Handle_Rod:1**, as shown in Figure 2–44 to zoom into the selection window.

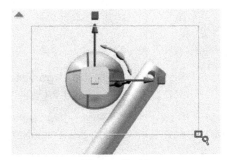

Figure 2–44

*With **Handle_Ball:1** selected, press <F> for a straight view of the hole.*

9. Using the Transform Handles, drag-and-drop the X- and Z-direction arrows so that **Handle_Ball:1** is placed over **Handle_Rod:1** and the hole in the ball matches the hole in the rod as shown in Figure 2–45.

10. Note that the base of the ball is toward the opposite end. To rotate **Handle_Ball:1**, select the Rotate transform handle (green arc) to open its heads-up edit box. Type **180.0** for the angle as shown in Figure 2–46. Press <Enter>.

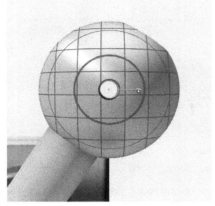
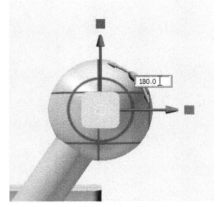

Figure 2–45   Figure 2–46

11. Using the mouse wheel, zoom out and pan to display the complete vise model. You can also click in empty space in the viewport to clear the selection and press <F> to fill the viewport with the complete model.

12. Note that a pin connects **Handle_Ball:2** and **Handle_Rod:1**. In the Organizer, in the Screw_Sub:1 part list, select **Pin:2**.

13. In the Menu Bar, select **Edit>Duplicate**. The pin is duplicated on top of the original one. It is also displayed in the Organizer, with the second **Pin:2** listed in the Screw_Sub:1 parts list.

14. In the Organizer, double-click on the second **Pin:2** and change its name to **Pin:1**, as shown in Figure 2–47. Press <Enter>.

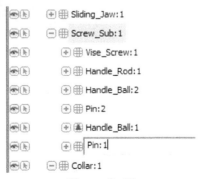

Figure 2–47

15. To move this new pin with **Handle_Ball:1**, copy and paste the transforms from **Handle_Ball** to the pin. Select **Handle_Ball:1** and select **Edit>Transform>Copy Transform**, as shown in Figure 2–48. Alternatively, you can press <Ctrl>+<Shift>+<C>.

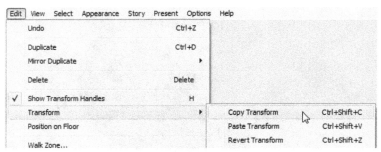

Figure 2–48

16. In the Organizer, select **Pin:1**. In the Menu Bar, select **Edit>Transform>Paste Transform**. The pin is moved to the correct location.

17. Click anywhere in empty space to clear selection.

18. Press <Alt> and click and drag to orbit around the Vise object. The completed vise displays similar to the one shown in Figure 2–49.

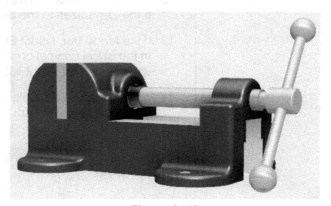

Figure 2–49

Task 3 - Organizing the objects.

In this task you will reorganize the parts in **Screw_Sub:1** by grouping the handle rod, two pins, two balls, and one part of **Vise_Screw:1** (**Vise_Screw:1_BODY-1**).

1. In the Organizer, under **Screw_Sub:1**, click  next to

   Vise_Screw:1 to display its parts list and click next to **Vise_Screw:1_BODY** to display its last hierarchy, as shown in Figure 2–50.

Figure 2–50

2. Verify nothing is selected, and then using <Ctrl>, select **Vise_Screw:1_BODY-1**, **Handle_Rod:1**, **Handle_Ball:1**,

   Handle_Ball:2, **Pin:1**, and **Pin:2** and click (Group), as shown in Figure 2–51.

3. A new group with the name **userGroup** is created in **Screw_Sub:1** and contains the selected objects. Double-click on *userGroup* and rename it as **Position_alt**, as shown in Figure 2–52. Press <Enter>.

Figure 2–51

Figure 2–52

4. Select **Position_alt** and note the parts selected in the viewport.

5. In the Menu Bar, select **File>Save As** to open the Save Scene As dialog box and save the scene as **myvise_transform.a3s**.

6. Close the Organizer by clicking **x**. Then, close the file by selecting **File>Close**.

Practice 2b

Adjusting and Visualizing a Scene

Practice Objectives

- Check and fix the surface normals.
- Set the **Ray Tracing** options and save the ray traced scene as an image file.

Estimated time for completion: 20 minutes

In this practice you will verify the orientation of the surface normals of the imported geometry and fix the ones that are reversed. You will also apply some visual styles and set the Ray tracing options to render the scene.

Task 1 - Verifying and fixing normals.

1. Click ![icon] (Your File) in the ![icon] (Open File) Task UI or select **File>Open**.

2. In the Open File dialog box, in your practice files folder, open the *Adjust_scene* folder, and select the file **Exterior_ Architectural_Model.fbx**. Click **Open**. An exterior architectural model is converted and loaded in the viewport. Close the Import Status dialog box. Note that some of the awnings and the front part of the wall display in black (as shown in Figure 2–53), indicating that the materials do not display correctly.

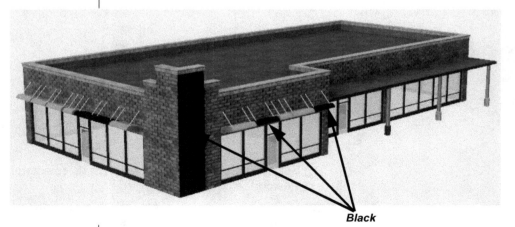

Black

Figure 2–53

3. The black areas indicate that the surface normals are not facing outward. Press <F7> to display the model in the Normals Visual style.

   • The parts with normals that are facing outward display in blue and the faces with normals facing inward (the incorrect orientation) display in yellow, as shown in Figure 2–54.

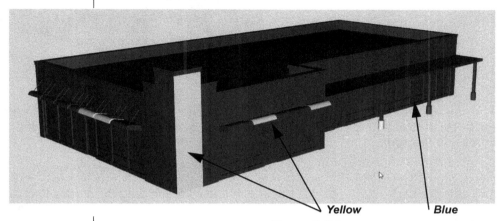

Yellow　　　*Blue*

Figure 2–54

4. Press <V> to open the Visual Styles interface. Note that in the *Diagnostic* category, the **Normals** swatch is selected (as shown in Figure 2–55), indicating that this visual style is currently assigned to the scene.

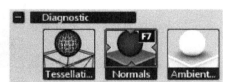

Figure 2–55

5. Press <V> again or click the **X** icon in the top right corner of the Visual Styles interface to close it.

6. Select **Options>Selection Display Style>White Wireframe** to change it so that it is clearly visible in the blue and yellow visual styles.

7. In the viewport, hold <Shift> and select the four yellow awnings, the front face of the wall (displayed in yellow), and the base of the pillar, as shown in Figure 2–56.

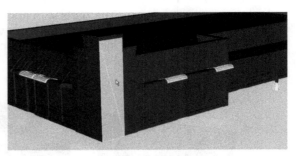

Figure 2–56

*You can also select **Edit>Reverse Normals** to reverse the normals.*

8. Press <F8> and note that the yellow parts display in blue, indicating that the normals have been reversed and are oriented correctly (facing outward).

9. Exit the selection by clicking in empty space.

You can also click

(Orbit) in the Navigation Bar. Press <Esc> to exit the command.

10. Hold <Alt> and click and drag the mouse to orbit around the model to verify that all of the faces have normals in the correct orientations.

11. At the back of the building, there is an awning and two small wall faces that display in yellow, as shown in Figure 2–57. Select the yellow faces and press <F8> to reverse them.

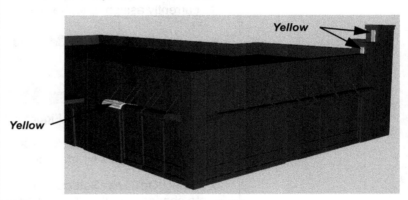

Figure 2–57

12. Exit the selection. In the ViewCube, click (Home) to orient to the front of the building. You might need to use a combination of **Zoom** and **Pan** to display the required orientation of the building, as shown in Figure 2–58.

13. Press <Esc> to exit the Normal visual style mode. Note that the brick material displays correctly on the wall and the awnings are not displayed in black, as shown in Figure 2–58.

Figure 2–58

Task 2 - Assigning visual styles.

---

1. Press <V> to open the Visual Styles interface. The **Both Shadows and Ambient Shadows** visual style swatch has a blue border indicating that it is currently being used, as shown in Figure 2–59.

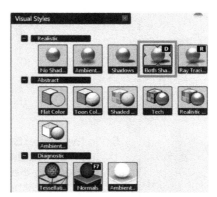

Figure 2–59

2. In the *Abstract* category, select the **Toon Color** swatch to display the building in a non-photorealistic visual style, as shown in Figure 2–60.

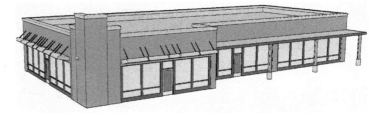

Figure 2–60

*Setting the **Render Levels** controls the number of levels to which the scene is rendered. When rendering a complex scene, set **Render Levels** or **Minutes** to render to specified levels or for a specific duration of time.*

3. Select **File>Settings>Performance and Quality** to open the Performance and Quality dialog box. Select the *Interactive Ray Tracing* tab.

4. At this stage you do not need to create a high-quality ray traced image. In the *Interactivity* area, drag the slider and set it as **30**. In the *Refine Image* area, select **For: render levels**, and type **10** in the edit box. In the Lighting Mode, clear the **Render shadows** option, as shown in Figure 2–61. Click **OK**.

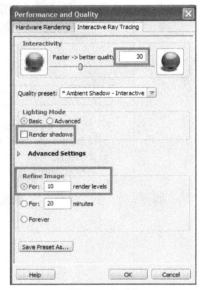

Figure 2–61

5. In the Visual Styles interface, in the *Realistic* category, select the **Ray Tracing** visual style swatch. The scene starts to render and the Ray Tracing Status interface (showing the progress) displays near the lower right corner of the viewport.

6. Because the Render Levels have been set to **10**, it can take a few minutes to complete the rendering. The rendered scene displays as shown in Figure 2–62.

Figure 2–62

7. In the Ray Tracing Status interface, once Ray Tracing has reached 100 %, click **Save** to open the Save Image As dialog box. Browse to your practice files folder and open the *Adjust_scene* folder. Save the image as a .JPG with the name **MyExterior_Architectural_Model_raytraced**.

8. In Windows Explorer, browse to your practice files folder and open the *Adjust_scene* folder. Note that **MyExterior_Architectural_Model_raytraced.xml** has been generated automatically along with the JPG file, as shown in Figure 2–63.

MyExterior_Architectural_Model_raytraced.jpg	9/9/2016 3:34 PM	JPEG Image	290 KB
MyExterior_Architectural_Model_raytraced.xml	9/9/2016 3:34 PM	XML Document	1 KB

Figure 2–63

*In the Adjust_scene folder, the **Exterior_Architectural_Model_raytraced.jpg** and its .XML file have also been provided for your reference.*

9. Double-click on **MyExterior_Architectural_Model_raytraced.jpg** to open it in an Image Viewer, as shown in Figure 2–64.

Figure 2–64

10. In the Autodesk Showcase viewport, save the scene as **MyExterior_Architectural_Model.a3s**.

11. Close the file.

Chapter Review Questions

1. Which of the following display styles is used in the scene shown in Figure 2-65?

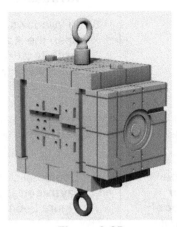

Figure 2-65

   a. Animated Grid

   b. White Wireframe

   c. Black Wireframe

   d. Blue Wireframe

2. Using the **Select All** option in the **Select** menu only enables you to select the geometry that displays in the scene. Hidden objects are not selected.

   a. True

   b. False

3. Which of the following icons in the Organizer toolbar can be used to hide a selected object in the viewport?

   a. ⊕

   b. ⊞

   c. 👁

   d. 👁

4. Once a model has been imported, it is important to verify that its surface normals are oriented correctly using <F7>. When checking a model, which color indicates that the normal is pointing outward correctly?

   a. Solid Yellow

   b. Yellow Cross-hairs

   c. Blue

   d. Blue Cross-hairs

5. Which of the following statements are true regarding transforming selected objects and their transformation handles? (Select all that apply.)

   a. The display of the transformation handles can be toggled by pressing <O>.

   b. Transformation handles can be used to translate and scale a selected object. They cannot be used to rotate.

   c. The Transformation dialog box can be used as an alternative to using the transformation handles for selected objects.

   d. Transforms can be copied between objects.

6. If a selected object was transformed previously, how do you transform it again so that it is transformed relative to its original location and not to the previously transformed location?

   a. Select the object and use the handles on the transform grip.

   b. Select the object and use the Transform Properties dialog box (**Edit>Transform>Transform Properties**).

   c. Select the object, open the Transform Properties dialog box (**Edit>Transform>Transform Properties**), and click **Transform....** to enter values in the Transform dialog box.

7. Match the following Transformation handle icons with their descriptions.

a. Enables you to move a selected object freely in any direction.

b. Enables you to rotate a selected object in a plane.

c. Enables you to scale a selected object evenly in all directions.

d. Enables you to drag a selected object translationally in one direction.

e. Enables you to scale a selected object in one direction.

8. Which of the following methods can be used to open the Visual Styles interface? (Select all that apply.)

a. Press <V>.

b. Press <Ctrl>+<V>.

c. Select **Appearance>Visual Styles Library**.

d. Click 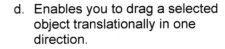 (Library) in the Visual Styles Task UI.

9. Which of the following are valid Visual Style categories in the Visual Styles interface? (Select all that apply.)

a. Visual Styles in Scene

b. Realistic

c. Abstract

d. Diagnostic

10. A rendering method is automatically set when a Visual Style is assigned.

a. True

b. False

Command Summary

Interface Component	Access Location
Organizer	• **Menu Bar:** Edit>Organizer • **Shortcut Key:** <O>
Transform Handles	• **Menu Bar:** Edit>Show Transform Handles • **Shortcut Key:** <H>
Visual Styles	• **Task UI:** Click (Visual Styles)> (Library) • **Menu Bar:** Appearance>Visual Style Library • **Shortcut Key:** <V>

Chapter

3

Setting the Scene

In this chapter you learn how to add Environments to a scene and how to enhance its lighting and shadow properties. You also learn how to incorporate accent lights into a scene for added brightness and to add materials to objects in the scene.

Learning Objectives in this Chapter

- Apply lighting environments and adjust the scene settings.
- Adjust the Environment lights and shadows.
- Add brightness to the scene by creating different types of accent light objects and control their properties.
- Manage, assign, replace, and modify the materials in the scene.
- Assign materials that contain different types of image maps applied to its parameters.
- Apply decal materials to objects on top of the already assigned materials.

Autodesk Showcase Workflow

Figure 3–1 shows the overall suggested workflow for the Autodesk® Showcase® software. The horizontal line at the top represents the high-level workflow and each of their sub-steps are detailed vertically below them. The highlighted column represents the content discussed in the current chapter.

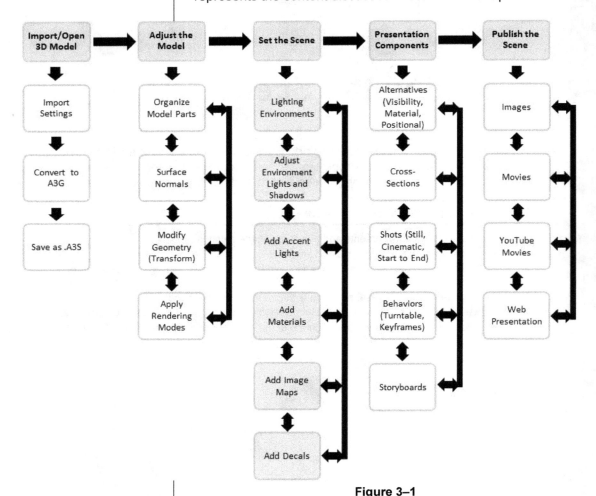

Figure 3–1

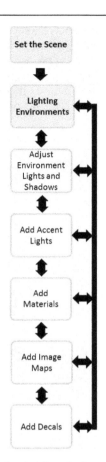

The Task UI only lists a few of the available environments.

3.1 Lighting Environments

The Autodesk Showcase software enables you to add an environment to visually enhance a scene. An environment adds a background and its associated lighting, shadows, highlights, and reflections to enhance the visual display of a model and improve realism. The background of the environment is a High Dynamic Range (HDR) image, which is a shape that completely surrounds the model.

Lighting environments are controlled using the Lighting Environments interface. To open/close this interface, select **Appearance>Lighting Environment Library** or press <E>. You can also open it by clicking ▦ (Library) in the Lighting Environments & Background Task UI (◠).

By default, the scene of a newly imported or opened model uses the Empty environment. You can apply an alternate environment using either of the following methods:

- Select a new environment swatch in the Lighting Environments & Background Task UI (◠) to assign it.

- Select an environment swatch in the Lighting Environment interface to assign it.

The Lighting Environment interface is divided into two categories: *Environments in Scene* and *Environment Libraries*. The *Environments in Scene* category lists the current and all previous environments that have been used in the scene.

The *Environment Libraries* category has an extensive list of additional environments that can be added to the scene. These are installed with the software. However, they must be added to the scene by selecting a swatch to add it to the *Environments in Scene* category for use in the scene. Figure 3–2 shows the two environment categories. The only environment in the scene is the default Empty environment.

If all of the rows of swatches are not visible, click the Up and Down arrows to scroll through the list. If the Environment Libraries list is not displayed, the scene is currently in Presentation mode. Press <Tab> to exit this mode.

Some of the available environments in the software have copyright restrictions. You have to arrange the copyright permissions if you want to use them for commercial purposes.

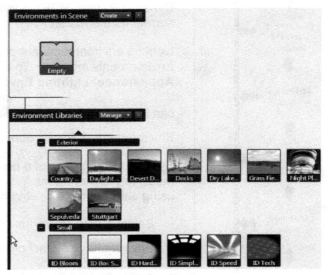

Figure 3–2

Hint: Creating Custom Environments

A custom lighting environment can be created using the Lighting Environments interface. In the *Environments in Scene* category, click **Create** and select the type of environment that you want to create, as shown in Figure 3–3. Once selected, you can assign custom settings in the Lighting Environment and Background Properties dialog box.

Figure 3–3

Hint: Adding Custom Environments

A custom lighting environment can be added to the Library and used in a scene. Click **Manage** and select **Add Library**, as shown in Figure 3–4. In the dialog box, browse and select the custom environment and then select its swatch to add it to the *Environments in Scene* category for use in the scene.

Figure 3–4

Adjusting the Scene

Scene settings can be adjusted in the applied environment to create a realistic visual display.

Hint: Setting Units

Before changing the scene settings, set the units in the software to match the units of the imported geometry. This makes it easier to modify the environment and to position the geometry with respect to the environment. Select **File> Settings>Scene Settings** to open the Scene Settings dialog box. In the *Units* area (shown in Figure 3–5), set the units to **Imperial** or **Metric** based on the imported geometry.

Figure 3–5

Scene Settings

The software enables you to modify the environment's characteristics with respect to the geometry. Select **File> Settings>Scene Settings** to open the Scene Settings dialog box. In the *Lighting Environment Properties* area (shown in Figure 3–6), you can modify the size and position of the environment with respect to the geometry.

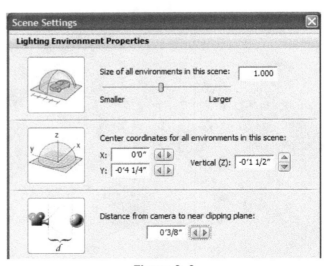

Figure 3–6

The changes in the Lighting Environment Properties are applied to all of the environments that are applied to the scene (active or not).

- **Size of all environments in this scene:** By default, the size of the environments is **1.0**, which means the environment is added at 1:1 scale with respect to the geometry. Select and drag the slider or enter a value to increase or decrease the environment size.

- **Center coordinates for all environments in this scene:** By default, the center of the environment matches the center of the scene. Enter new values in the *X*, *Y*, and *Z* edit boxes to position the environment with respect to the scene geometry.

Setting Floor Position

When geometry is imported into a scene it might not be correctly placed on the floor. The floor position can be set by moving the geometry or moving the environment's floor, as follows:

- Select the objects that you want to move on top of the floor, and select **Edit>Position on Floor**, as shown in Figure 3–7. All of the selected objects are automatically moved to sit on top of the environment's floor.

Figure 3–7

- Select **Edit>Set Environment Floor Position** (as shown in Figure 3–7) to open the Set Floor position dialog box.

- In the Set Floor position dialog box, use the slider to move the environment floor up or down to adjust it with respect to the geometry, as shown in Figure 3–8. You can also enter a specific value and move the environment floor along the Z-axis. You can also click **Move to Bottom of 3D Model** to move the environment floor to the bottom of the lowest object in the scene.

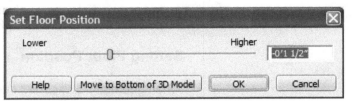

Figure 3–8

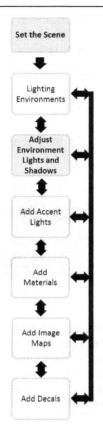

Set the Scene

↓

Lighting Environments ↔

↕

Adjust Environment Lights and Shadows ↔

↕

Add Accent Lights ↔

↕

Add Materials ↔

↕

Add Image Maps ↔

↕

Add Decals ↔

3.2 Environment Lights and Shadows

The Lighting Environments available in the Autodesk Showcase software include lights and shadows. You can control both lights and shadows to achieve the required effect. Lights brighten the scene and the model geometry in the scene. Lights and shadows are critical for producing highly realistic visualizations.

Each lighting environment uses two types of lights: an IBL (image-based light) and an environment light. The IBL is set based on the environment and cannot be modified. It provides overall brightness to a scene and the objects. Environment light is a directional light that casts parallel rays that brighten areas of an object where the rays hit and cast shadows on the ground where the object is blocking the light rays. You can control the settings of the environment light to brighten the objects or cast shadows, as shown in Figure 3–9.

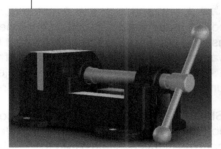
No environment light

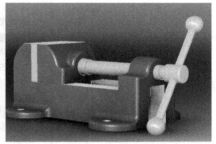
Environment light with no shadows

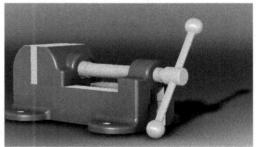
Environment light with shadows

Figure 3–9

Adjusting Environment Light and Shadows

The Task UI is generally used for simple modifications, such as moving the directional light or shadows.

To make a scene more realistic, you might need to adjust the environment light and the shadows that it casts. To do so, you can use the Task UI or the Directional Light and Shadows dialog box.

Using the Adjust Lighting Task UI

In the Task UI, click  (Adjust Lighting) to open the Adjust Lighting panel, as shown in Figure 3–10.

Figure 3–10

Click (Light) and click and drag the cursor anywhere in the viewport to move the directional light of the environment. Release the cursor to set the environment light in this position. If you want to move the highlight on the surface of the geometry, press <Ctrl> and click and drag on the object surface. Release the cursor to set the highlight in this position. Similarly, click

 (Shadow) and click and drag the cursor anywhere in the viewport to move the scene shadows. Release the cursor to set the shadows in this position. Drag the Brightness Level slider bar from dark to bright (left to right) to set the global exposure in the scene.

The Directional Light and Shadows Dialog Box

The Directional Light and Shadows dialog box is used for more extensive modifications to the directional light of the active environment and to modify shadow properties for all environments.

The Directional Light and Shadows dialog box provides more detailed control, rather than only controlling placement. Select **Appearance>Directional Light and Shadows** to open the Directional Light and Shadows dialog box, as shown in Figure 3–11.

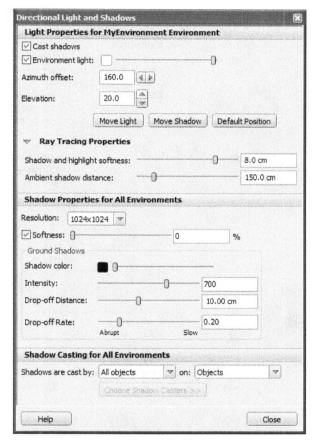

Figure 3–11

The dialog box contains three areas that enable you to control the directional light of the active environment, shadow properties, and shadow casting universally for all of the environments.

Light Properties for the Active Environment

Cast Shadows	Control whether the directional light should cast shadows in the scene. The *Shadow Properties* and *Shadow Casting* areas are disabled if the **Cast Shadows** option is cleared.
Environment light	Set the environment light as ON or OFF. Use ☐ to set the color of the light and use the slider to increase or decrease the brightness.
Azimuth	Move the environment light horizontally in the environment dome. Use the left or right arrows or enter an angle between 0 to 360.
Elevation	Move the environment light vertically between the floor and the top point of the environment dome. Use the up and down arrows or enter an angle between -90 to 90.
Move Light	Move the environment light vertically or horizontally by clicking **Move Light**. In the viewport, click and drag the cursor in the required direction. You can also move the highlight on the surface of the geometry by holding <Ctrl> and selecting the surface of the model. Click **Stop Moving** when done. This is same as using the **Light** tool in the Adjust Lighting Task UI.
Move Shadow	Enables you to move the shadow by clicking **Move Shadow**. In the viewport, click and drag the cursor in the required direction. Click **Stop Moving** when done. This is same as using the **Shadow** tool in the Adjust Lighting Task UI.
Default Position	Move the directional light to its original position in that environment.
Ray Tracing Properties	Control the shadow and highlight softness and ambient shadow distance in Ray Tracing, which is created for that environment light.

*This area is only active if **Cast Shadows** is selected in the Light Properties for Active Environment area.*

Shadow Properties for All Environments

Resolution	Set the resolution of the shadows. If you increase the shadow resolution, it might decrease the performance. A resolution of 1024X1024 is recommended. You can increase the resolution at the time of presentation to create high-quality shadows.
Softness	Set the shadows to be soft or sharp.

Shadows: sharp   *Shadows: soft*

Shadow Color	Control the shadow color.
Intensity	Increase or decrease the color strength of the shadow.
Drop-off Distance	Controls the intensity of the shadows based on the distance between the object and the ground.
Drop-off Rate	Controls the intensity of the shadows based on the distance between the directional light and the object.

*This area is only active if **Cast Shadows** is selected in the Light Properties for Active Environment area.*

Shadow Casting for All Environments

Shadow are Cast by:	Select **All objects** that cast a shadow or only **Specified objects** that cast a shadow.
Shadow are Cast on:	Select **Objects**, **Ground**, or **Ground and objects** on which the shadows are being cast.
Choose Shadow Casters	If you selected **Specified objects** in **Shadow are Cast by**, **Choose Shadow Casters>>** activates and displays different options that can cast shadows.

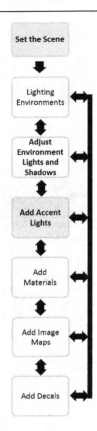

Set the Scene

Lighting
Environments

Adjust
Environment
Lights and
Shadows

Add Accent
Lights

Add
Materials

Add Image
Maps

Add Decals

3.3 Accent Lights

Accent Lights add illumination to the model and the space around it to make the scene brighter, add highlights, or create drama.

Two types of accent lights available:

- **Selective Spot Light:** Casts focused beams of light in a cone with a circular base.

- **Selective Point Light:** Casts light equally in all directions.

For an accent light to affect the scene it must be associated with an object(s). Any unassociated objects remain unchanged. You can associate an object with an accent light as follows:

How To: Create an Accent Light Associated with an Object

1. Select **Appearance>Accent Lights** or press <L>. The Accent Lights interface opens.
2. Select an object(s) in the viewport to be associated with the accent light.
3. In the Accent Lights interface, click **Create** and select the type of accent light you want to add in the scene, as shown in Figure 3–12.

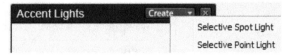

Figure 3–12

The light grips are similar to any other object in the viewport and can be named, moved, rotated, and edited.

An image representing the selected light is added to the Accent Light interface and its associated light object grip (displayed in yellow) is placed in the viewport, as shown in Figure 3–13.

***Spot Light
Image and Grip***   ***Point Light
Image and Grip***

Figure 3–13

4. Rename the accent light so that it has a name relevant to the scene or object being accented. To rename it, in the Accent Lights interface, double-click on the name **Spot** or **Point** and type the new name in the accent light's swatch.

If the transform handles for the accent light's grip do not display when selected, press <H> to display them.

5. Move or rotate the accent light, as required. Select the corresponding accent light's grip, and use the handles shown in Figure 3–14 to translate or rotate the accent light.

Transform Light
Figure 3–14

Press <O> to open the Organizer if not already done.

6. Use the Organizer shown in Figure 3–15, to hide or unhide an accent light.

Organizer list
Figure 3–15

To associate additional selected objects to an existing accent light, use either of the following:

- Right-click on the accent light and select **Add Selection To** as shown in Figure 3–16.

Figure 3–16

- In the Accent Light interface, double-click on the accent light to open its Accent Light Properties dialog box. Next to **Associated objects**, click **Choose>>** and select **Add Selection To** as shown in Figure 3–17.

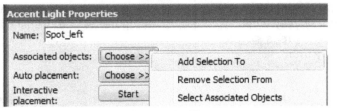

Figure 3–17

Hint: Modifying Accent Light Grips

Right-click on the light grip and select **Hide Accent Light Grips** or **Set Accent Light Grips Size** (as shown in Figure 3–18), to hide the light grips in the viewport or change their sizes. These options do not remove or change the light.

Figure 3–18

You can also hide/unhide the accent light grips by selecting **Option>Show Accent Light Grips**, or by pressing <Shift>+<L>.

Accent Light Properties

An accent light must be selected for options to be displayed in the Accent Light Properties dialog box.

The Accent Light Properties dialog box (shown in Figure 3–19), controls the light settings and how the lights brighten the associated objects. To open this dialog box use one of the following methods:

- Double-click on the accent light image in the Accent light interface.

- Right-click on the accent light image and select **Properties**.

- Select the accent light and select **Appearance>Accent Light Properties**. Select the accent light to display its properties in the dialog box.

- Select the accent light and press <Ctrl>+<L>. Select the accent light to display its properties in the dialog box.

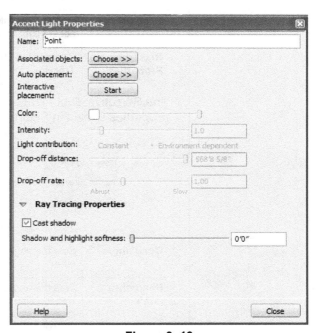

Figure 3–19

The Accent Light Properties for the Spot light and Point light are the same, with a few additional options for the Spot light properties.

Use the following options to modify the settings of an accent lights:

Associated objects	Clicking **Choose >>** enables you to add and remove selected objects to or from the accent light. It can also be used to select and highlight objects that are associated with the light.
Auto Placement	Click **Choose >>** to automatically place the accent light in front of, behind, or above the associated objects.
Interactive placement	Moves the light in the viewport. Click **Start** and click and drag the cursor to move the accent light. Use <Ctrl> and click to place the highlight.
Color	Uses ☐ to set the color of the light and use the slider to change the hue of the color.
Intensity	Increases or decreases the brightness of the light. You can enter a value from -10 to +10 to define its brightness.

Light contribution	Sets the intensity of the light based on the environment. Brighter lights in brighter environments and lighter lights in darker environments.
Drop-off distance	Controls the distance between the accent light and the associated object. If the accent light is farther than the specified distance, the light does not affect the object.
Drop-off rate	Controls the intensity based on the distance between the accent light and the associated object.
Ray Tracing Properties	Controls the shadow and highlight softness in Ray Tracing.

The Selective Spot Light accent light provides the additional properties shown in Figure 3–20.

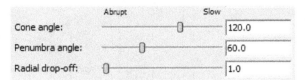

Figure 3–20

Cone angle	Sets the angle from one edge of the spot light beam to the other.
Penumbra angle	Sets the angle from one edge of the drop off to the other. Use the slider or enter a value. In the figure below, the inner circle is the penumbra angle and the outer circle is the cone angle. The light fades from full intensity to zero intensity between these angles. Therefore, when these angles have similar values, the light creates a sharply defined pool of light. When the angles are widely separated, the angles create a soft, gradual fade. The penumbra angle has to be equal to or smaller than the cone angle.
Radial drop-off	Sets the rate for the drop-off of intensity from the center to the outer edge of the cone. Use the slider or enter a value.

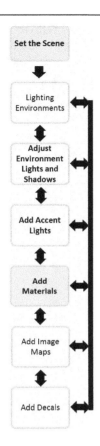

3.4 Materials

Creating believable visualizations almost always involves adding materials to geometry so that it resembles real-world objects. Materials control the color, texture, transparency, and other physical properties. Materials also control how light interacts with surfaces in 3D models. The surfaces of the models in the viewport interact with the light sources based on the material assignments. If an object is shiny, it reflects the light. With transparency applied, the light passes through the object.

Materials are managed by the Materials interface, as shown in Figure 3–21. It lists all of the materials present in the scene and those included in the software's Material Library. To open the Materials interface, select **Appearance>Materials Library** or press <M>. Alternatively, use the Task UI by clicking ◐ (Look) and clicking ▣ (Materials) in the Look panel.

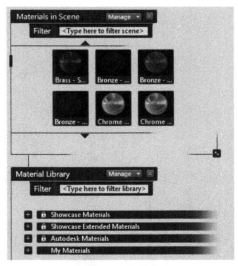

Figure 3–21

The Materials interface has the two main categories: *Materials in Scene* and *Material Library*.

Materials in Scene

All materials that have been used in the scene display as swatches in the *Materials in Scene* category. Use the left scroll bar or the up and down arrows shown in Figure 3–22 to scroll through the list of scene materials. Click and drag 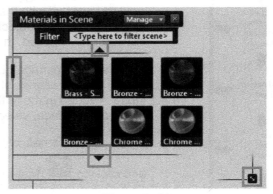 in the bottom right corner of the *Materials in Scene* category to dynamically resize the area.

Figure 3–22

The symbols displayed in a material's swatch identify the state of the material in the scene. The symbols are as follows:

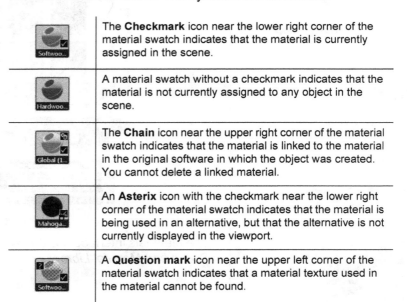

	The **Checkmark** icon near the lower right corner of the material swatch indicates that the material is currently assigned in the scene.
	A material swatch without a checkmark indicates that the material is not currently assigned to any object in the scene.
	The **Chain** icon near the upper right corner of the material swatch indicates that the material is linked to the material in the original software in which the object was created. You cannot delete a linked material.
	An **Asterix** icon with the checkmark near the lower right corner of the material swatch indicates that the material is being used in an alternative, but that the alternative is not currently displayed in the viewport.
	A **Question mark** icon near the upper left corner of the material swatch indicates that a material texture used in the material cannot be found.

Managing Scene Materials

You can manage scene materials using the options in the right-click shortcut menu, as shown in Figure 3–23.

The options in the right-click shortcut menu vary depending on the material.

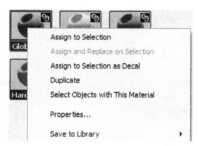

Figure 3–23

*The **Assign to Selection** option is not available if an object has not been selected.*

- Once an object is selected, right-click on the material to be assigned, and select **Assign to Selection**.

- When creating a custom material it is recommended that you select an existing material with similar characteristics to the new one that is required, right-click and select **Duplicate**. Once the custom material has been created, rename it, and change the material's properties, as required, using the **Properties** option to open the Material Properties dialog box.

- A modified or custom material from the scene can be saved in the Library for use in another scene. To do so, right-click on the material and select **Save to Library**.

Filtering Scene Materials

Materials that are listed in the *Materials in Scene* category can be filtered so that the list only displays materials that match a defined requirement. To filter materials, in the *Materials in Scene* category bar, click **Manage** as shown in Figure 3–24, and select the filter type. As an alternative, you can enter text in the *Filter* field to filter the list by name.

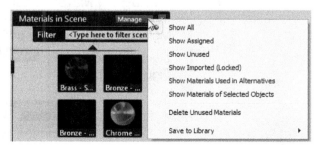

Figure 3–24

Material Library

The *Material Library* category contains the list of libraries and their associated materials, that are available in the Autodesk Showcase software. The *Material Library* category is shown in Figure 3–25. Click ⊞ next to a material library to expand its lists and click ⊟ to collapse them. Use the left scroll bar or the up and down arrows to scroll through any of the expanded lists of materials.

Custom Autodesk Inventor Libraries are not imported and not listed in the Material Library category for use in the Autodesk Showcase software. Materials that were used in a custom library in the Inventor model are imported and listed in the Materials in Scene category.

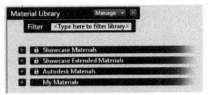

Figure 3–25

Types of Materials

Different types of materials are available in the Autodesk Showcase software and categorized into different libraries.

- **Showcase Materials:** Created specifically for the Autodesk Showcase software and are highly customizable.

- **Showcase Extended Materials:** Created specifically for the Autodesk Showcase software and are highly customizable. Provides an expanded list of materials to those available in the Showcase Materials library.

- **Autodesk Materials:** Common across multiple Autodesk software (Autodesk Revit, AutoCAD, Autodesk Inventor, Autodesk 3ds Max, etc). When importing objects from these products into the Autodesk Showcase software, the materials display as they did in their originating software products. These materials are based on real-world parameters.

Managing Material Library

Material libraries can be added and removed. In the *Material Library* category, click **Manage ▼** to display the menu, as shown in Figure 3–26.

Figure 3–26

Select **Add Library** to open a dialog box, browse, and select a folder location in which a new library is created. Once a library has been created, you can save the custom materials from the *Materials in Scene* category to it. Right-click on the required material and select **Save to Library**. The **Remove Library** option enables you to remove a library from the *Material Library* category for the current scene, but it does not delete the materials or the library from its folder location.

Assigning Materials

Materials can be assigned to objects from the *Materials in Scene* or *Material Library* categories.

Once a material has been assigned it remains in the Materials in Scene category, even if it is not being used.

- **Assign Material from Materials in Scene:** You can assign a material that is listed in the *Materials in Scene* category by selecting the object or multiple objects in the viewport and selecting the material to be assigned. Alternatively, you can select the object, right-click on the material, and select **Assign to Selection**.

If an object is not selected before selecting a material swatch in the Material Library, the material is listed in the Materials in Scene category but is not assigned to any object.

- **Assign Material from Material Library:** Materials can also be assigned directly from the Material Library by selecting the object or multiple objects in the viewport, and selecting the material. Alternatively, you can select the object, right-click on the material and select **Assign to Selection**. Note that the selected material is also added to the *Materials in Scene* category and displays a checkmark in its swatch indicating that it is being used in the current scene.

- **Copy assigned materials to objects:** Materials can also be copied between objects. In the viewport, select the object whose material you want to assign to another object, select **Appearance>Copy Material** or press <Shift>+<C> to copy the material. Select the object or objects (use <Shift> for selecting multiple objects) to assign the same material and select **Appearance>Paste Material** or press <Shift>+<V>.

Replacing Materials

When importing objects, review how the materials are imported to verify that they display correctly or replace them with an Autodesk Showcase material.

After importing objects into the Autodesk Showcase software, you might want to change the imported materials for better display and visualization or keep the originating software's assign materials.

Imported materials can be replaced by selecting **Appearance> Replace Materials** to open the Replace Imported Materials dialog box, as shown in Figure 3–27.

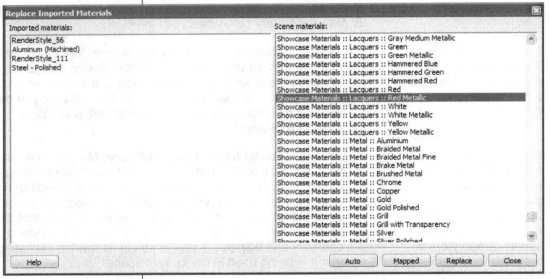

Figure 3–27

Use any of the following techniques to replace an imported material:

- Select an imported material in the *Imported Materials* column in the dialog box and select a material in the *Scene materials* area. Click **Replace**. The material is removed from the dialog box and applied to the object in the viewport. It is also listed in the *Materials in Scene* category in the Materials interface.

- Click **Auto** to automatically replace the imported materials with materials with similar names.

- Click **Mapped** to replace the materials using custom mapping algorithm files.

Hint: Cleaning Materials in Scene Category

After assigning and replacing materials, there might be a number of unused materials in the scene. It is a good practice to delete unused materials.

- To individually delete used materials, right-click and select **Delete**, as shown in Figure 3–28.

Figure 3–28

- To delete all of the unused materials at the same time, click **Manage** in the *Materials in Scene* category and select **Delete Unused Materials**, as shown in Figure 3–29.

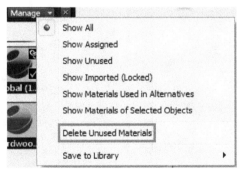

Figure 3–29

Material Properties

Materials can be modified to adjust their individual properties. The properties that can be modified are specific to each material and listed in the Material Properties dialog box, as shown in Figure 3–30. To open the Material Properties dialog box, double-click on the material or right-click and select **Properties**. Alternatively, in the viewport, right-click on the object whose material properties you want to modify, and select **Material Properties** or select an object and select **Appearance>Material Properties**.

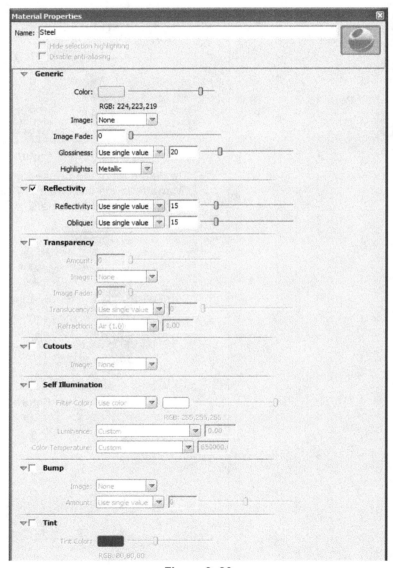

Figure 3–30

The properties in the Material Properties dialog box vary with the type of material. These parameters can be modified to enhance a material and how they display in the scene. Some of the commonly available parameters are as follows:

Color parameters	Use to enhance the look of the material in different lighting. You can also use an image to display on the selected surface, such as a wood texture image that can be used on the floor geometry.
Reflectivity	How an object reflects the environment and other objects.
Highlight	Controls the shiny spots on the surface where the light is reflected from the object.
Clear Coat Highlight	Used for car paints, which has an extra coat of shininess and reflectivity. Use this parameter to add additional shininess.
Transparency	Sets the transparency or opacity of your material.
Decal	Uses an image to determine their look. These decal materials can be applied on top of other materials.
Bump	Adds indentations and roughness in the visibility of a material.

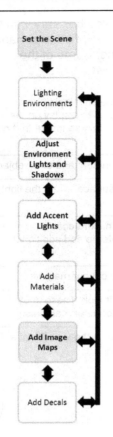

Set the Scene

Lighting Environments

Adjust Environment Lights and Shadows

Add Accent Lights

Add Materials

Add Image Maps

Add Decals

3.5 Image Maps

The key components of materials are image maps that add a real world visual effect to an object. Image maps are based on 2D image files and can be in a .JPG, .BMP, .TIFF, or .PNG format. Materials can include multiple image maps to serve different purposes. Image maps cannot be applied directly to objects in a scene. They are assigned to materials instead. These materials are then applied to objects, as shown in Figure 3–31.

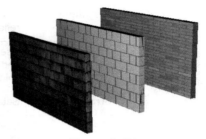

Figure 3–31

Maps can be used for different parameters in a material. Image maps can be applied to a material parameter in the Material Properties dialog box, as shown in Figure 3–32.

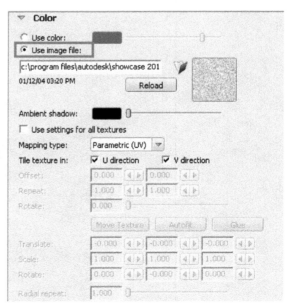

Figure 3–32

The parameters to which image maps can be applied, include the following:

- **Color maps:** Often the most important when creating realistic materials. These images replace the solid color of the material and can be repeated over the surface of the object.

Reflection map is only used during Hardware renderings and has no affect in Ray Tracing.

- **Reflection maps:** Images that are used to reflect from the object surface. In the Autodesk Showcase software, the default for the reflection map is the environment that has been assigned. You can assign an image to be applied as a reflection map instead of the environment's map.

- **Transparency maps:** Controls whether specific parts are transparent and others are opaque, as shown with the lace curtains in Figure 3–33. The black to white values are mapped to the transparent state, in which white creates a hole (completely invisible) and black creates a surface (100% opaque). Grays create a semi-transparent affect, which is good for clouds or fabrics. If a color image is used as an opacity map, the RGB color is ignored and only the Luminance value is used.

Figure 3–33

- **Bump maps:** Creates the illusion of an embossed or pitted surface without having actual geometry present on the model, as shown for a braided carpet in Figure 3–34.

Figure 3–34

- **Decal maps:** Used with decal materials and provide a shape and transparency. It is similar to a transparency map, but can be placed on top of another material.

How To: Apply Image Maps

1. Select the surface or objects to which you want to apply an image map.
2. Open the Material interface (press <M>) and apply a material to it, if not already applied.
3. Double-click on the material's swatch, in the *Materials in Scene* category, to open its Material Properties dialog box.
4. Locate the parameter to which you want to apply the image map, and select **Use image file**, as shown in Figure 3–35.

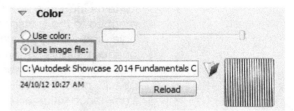

Figure 3–35

5. Click 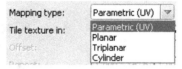 and browse to the folder in which the image file is located. Select and open the image file.
6. Use the **Mapping type** option, as shown in Figure 3–36.

Figure 3–36

- Select **Parametric (UV)** to map the image along the UV coordinates of the selected surface.
- Select **Planar** to project the image onto the surface in a single direction.
- Select **Triplanar** to project the image onto the surface from three sides.
- Select **Cylinder** to project the image so that it is rolled onto the surface.

7. In *Tile texture in*, select the tiling option. This enables you to repeat the texture horizontally, vertically, or both horizontally and vertically. Clear **U direction** and **V direction** to project the image in a single direction.

8. Use the **Offset**, **Repeat**, and **Rotate** options to manually control the repetition of the image on the surface.

9. To place the image at the right location on the surface you can either:

    • Use **Autofit** to automatically align the image in the bounding box of the selected surface.

    • To manually move the image to the required location, click **Move Texture**. This displays the transform handles for the image in the viewport. You can use the transform handles to move, scale, and rotate the image map into position. Once the image map is at the required location, click **Stop Moving**. Alternatively, you can enter the correct number in the edit boxes, as shown in Figure 3–37.

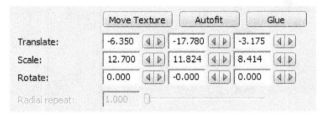

Figure 3–37

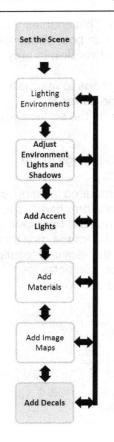

3.6 Decal Materials

Labels, logos, or artwork can be added to objects in a scene. This is done using a special material called a *Decal*. The Decal material contains an image file that represents the label, logo, or artwork. The object's Material remains assigned and the Decal material is added on top of it. Once assigned to an object, the Decal Material can be manipulated and moved to the required location on the object. Predefined Decal Materials are located in **Showcase Materials>***Decals* category in the Materials Library, as shown in Figure 3–38. You can use any one of these decals as a base for creating a custom decal for your scene.

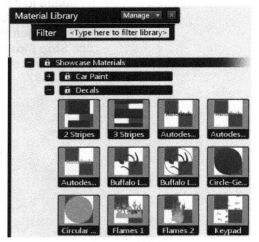

Figure 3–38

Once a decal has been applied to an object, ⭐ (Decal Grip) displays at the center of the decal material on the object. You can use the decal grip to transform the decals similar to how other objects are transformed in the scene. As with other materials, you can modify the properties of a decal's material using the Material Properties dialog box.

How To: Create and Assign a Decal Material

1. In the Material interface, select a Decal material in the Showcase Materials library to add it to the *Materials in Scene* category.
2. Select the object to which you want to apply the decal material, right-click on the material to be assigned, and select **Assign to Selection as Decal**.
3. Double-click on the decal material to open its Material Properties dialog box.

4. In the *Decal* area, click  and browse to the folder in which the decal image file is located. Select and open the decal image file. Note that **Use 'Decal' image file** is already selected, as shown in Figure 3–39. Click **Reload**.

Figure 3–39

5. Similar to applying an image file in any other material, set the **Mapping type** and **Tile texture in** options, as required.

If a Decal Material has been applied behind an object, use the shortcut menu to obtain a list of available decals for ease of selection.

6. In the viewport, click ✦ (Decal Grip), if not already selected.
7. Click **Move Texture** to display the transform handles on the decal grip and use the transforms to place the decal at the required location.
8. Modify the other properties, such as the **Color**, **Reflectivity & Highlight**, **Transparency**, **Bump**, etc., as required.

Hint: Changing the Color of a Decal Grip

To change the color of a displayed Decal Grip in your model, edit the Properties of the Decal Material, expand the Decal Grip Properties area, and use the slider to change the color.

Practice 3a

Adding a Lighting Environment

Practice Objectives

- Assign and adjust the size, lighting, and brightness of a lighting environment in the scene.
- Adjust the environment floor.

Estimated time for completion: 30 minutes

In this practice you will add a Lighting Environment and then adjust its lights and brightness. You will also adjust the environment floor, so that the base of the object lies on top of it.

Task 1 - Assigning a lighting environment.

1. Click ▨ (Your File) in the 📁 (Open File) Task UI or select **File>Open**.

2. In the Open File dialog box, browse to the *Vise_Environment* folder of your practice files folder.

3. Select **Vise.iam**. Do not open the file.

Default shots can be created using the Import Settings dialog box. You can modify or delete them in the Shots interface.

4. In the Open File dialog box, click **Settings...** to open the Import Settings dialog box. In the *3D Model* tab, verify that *Conversion setting* is set to **001-All Purpose**. In the *New Scene Lighting Style* area, open the list of available environments and select **Empty**, if required, as shown in Figure 3–40. When you open the file, it uses the Empty Lighting Environment.

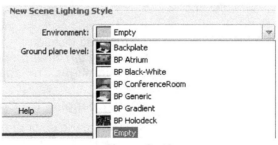

Figure 3–40

5. Close the Import Settings dialog box and open the file **Vise.iam**.

6. In the Inventor Assembly Settings dialog box, click **Continue** to load the file. After loading, the vise displays as a new scene in the viewport, as shown in Figure 3–41.

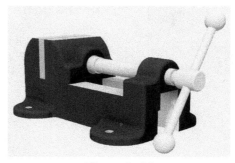

Figure 3–41

7. Close the Import Status dialog box, if open.

8. Select **Appearance>Lighting Environment Library** or press <E> to toggle on the display of the Lighting Environment interface.

   • In the *Environments in Scene* category, note that **Empty** displays and is surrounded by a blue border indicating that it is currently in use, as shown in Figure 3–42.

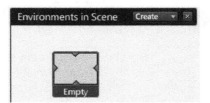

Figure 3–42

9. In the *Environment Libraries* category, expand the **Geometry Background>***Small* category. Select the **ID Bloom** environment, as shown in Figure 3–43.

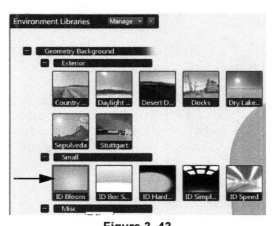

Figure 3–43

10. The **ID Bloom** environment is now listed in the *Environments in Scene* category and surrounded by a blue border indicating that it is the active environment. Note how the light is falling on the vise and how the shadows display, as shown in Figure 3–44. Press <E> to toggle off the Environments interface.

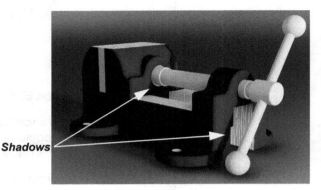

Shadows

Figure 3–44

Task 2 - Adjust the lighting environment.

1. Using the mouse wheel, zoom out until the lighting environment dome with the vise sitting in the center, displays as shown in Figure 3–45.

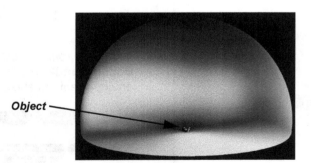

Object

Figure 3–45

2. Select **File>Settings>Scene Settings** to open the Scene Settings dialog box.

3. In the *Units* area, set the *Format* to **Imperial** and *Units* to **Feet & Fractional Inches**, if required, as shown in Figure 3–46.

Figure 3–46

4. In the *Lighting Environment Properties* area, for **Size of all environments in this scene**, click and slowly drag the slider toward the left (Smaller) until the edit box displays a value of something close to **0.500**, as shown in Figure 3–47. The size of the environment dome is reduced and is more suitable for the vise model.

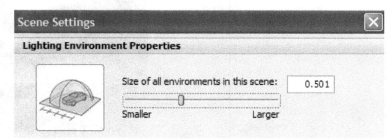

Figure 3–47

5. Click **OK** to close the Scene Settings dialog box.

6. In the Navigation Bar, click ⌕ (Zoom Fit All) to fill the viewport with the vise model.

7. In the Task UI, click ⬤ (Adjust Lighting) to display the Adjust Lighting panel.

8. Click 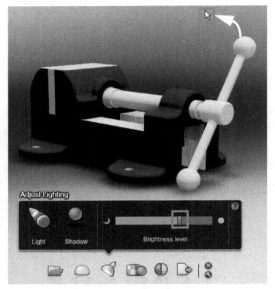 (Light). Starting from the upper ball, by clicking and holding on the upper ball of the handle and then dragging the cursor slightly left and up, as shown in Figure 3–48. Note how the highlights and shadows move in the environment. Release the cursor.

9. The object looks too bright. Drag the Brightness level slider bar slightly left to reduce the brightness, as shown in Figure 3–48.

Figure 3–48

10. Press <Esc> to exit the lighting adjustment. In the Task UI, click ⊗ to close the Adjust Lighting panel.

Task 3 - Adjust the environment's floor.

1. In the ViewCube, select the **FRONT** label. The vise displays in the Front view as shown in Figure 3–49. Note that the vise model is floating over the environment's floor (the white line).

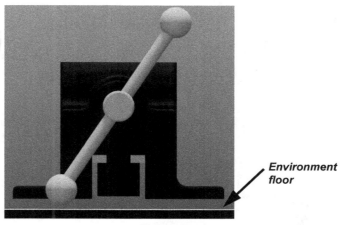

Environment floor

Figure 3–49

You can also select
Edit>Organizer *to open the Organizer.*

To change the Selection Display Style, select
Options>Selection Display Style*, and select a style.*
Animated Grid *is used in the images shown in Figure 3–50.*

2. The lower ball in the vise's screw subassembly will extend below the environment's floor if the model is repositioned on the floor. You are required to rotate the screw subassembly to prevent this. Press <O> to open the Organizer.

3. Expand **Vise.iam>Screw_Sub:1** and select **Screw_Sub:1**. Note that all of the objects in **Screw_Sub:1** are selected in the Organizer and in the viewport, as shown in Figure 3–50.

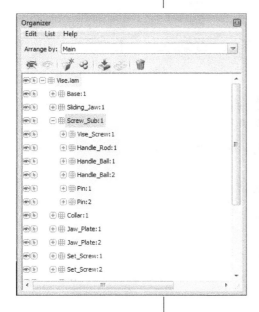

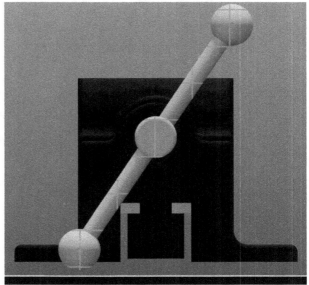

Figure 3–50

4. Select **Edit>Show Transform Handles** or press <H> to display the transform handles, if not already visible. Using the Rotate handle, slightly rotate the subassembly so that the lower ball is above the base of the vise, as shown in Figure 3–51.

5. Close the Organizer and press <Esc> to exit the selection.

6. Select **Edit>Set Environment Floor Position** to open the Set Floor Position dialog box.

7. Move the slider to the right (Higher) until the environment floor touches the base of the vise, as shown in Figure 3–52. Click **OK**.

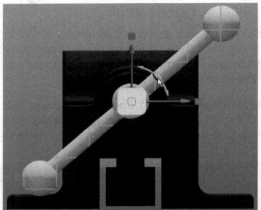

Figure 3–51   Figure 3–52

The units displayed in the Set Floor Position dialog box depend on the units specified in the Scene Settings dialog box, not on the model units. The two units can be different.

8. In the ViewCube, click 🏠 (Home) to orient the model to the original import position.

9. Save the file as **MyVise_Environment.a3s**.

Practice 3b

Materials and Decals

Practice Objectives

Estimated time for completion: 30 minutes

- Replace the imported materials with Autodesk materials and Showcase materials.
- Apply an image map and a decal map.

In this practice you will replace the imported materials that are still linked to the originating software with Autodesk and Showcase materials. You will apply an image map and modify the settings. Additionally you will apply a decal map to mask a logo to the object.

Task 1 - Replacing materials.

Alternatively in the Task UI, click  (Look) to open the Look panel and click

 *(Materials).*

If the material swatches are not visible in the interface, use

 *(Resize) to expand the interface area.*

1. Click ▨ (Your File) in the 📂 (Open File) Task UI or select **File>Open**.

2. In the Open File dialog box, browse to the *Vise_Material* folder of your practice files folder. Select and open **Vise_Material.a3s**.

3. Select **Appearance>Material Library** or press <M> to display the Materials interface. In the *Materials in Scene* category, five materials are listed. The swatches for these materials display the **Chain** icon, as shown in Figure 3–53. It indicates that the materials are linked to the original software in which the 3D model was created. In this case they are linked to the Autodesk® Inventor® software.

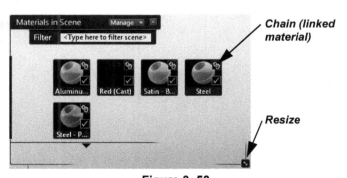

Figure 3–53

If the imported material names listed in the dialog box do not match the names in the Materials interface, open the Material Properties dialog box to verify the corresponding names.

4. Select **Appearance>Replace Materials** to open the Replace Imported Materials dialog box. Note the five materials listed in the *Imported materials* area, as shown in Figure 3–54.

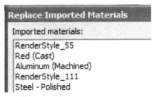

Figure 3–54

5. Select **Appearance>Material Properties** or press <Ctrl>+<M> to open the Material Properties dialog box.

6. In the Replace Imported Materials dialog box, in the *Imported materials* area, select each material and note its corresponding name in the Material Properties dialog box. For example, **RenderStyle_55** corresponds to **Aluminum - Polished,** as shown in Figure 3–55.

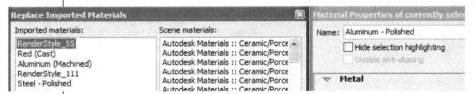

Figure 3–55

7. In the Replace Imported Materials dialog box, in the *Imported materials* area, select **RenderStyle_55**. In the *Scene materials* area, select **Showcase Materials::Metal:: Aluminium** and click **Replace**, as shown in Figure 3–56.

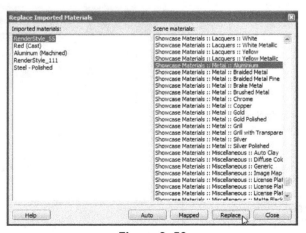

Figure 3–56

8. Replace the remaining linked materials with their corresponding Autodesk materials, as follows:

- **Red (Cast):** Autodesk Materials::Metal/Aluminum:: Anodized - Red
- **Aluminum (Machined):** Autodesk Materials:: Metal/Steel::Machined03
- **RenderStyle_111:** Autodesk Materials:: Metal/Steel:: Stainless - Polished
- **Steel-Polished:** Autodesk Materials:: Metal/Steel:: Stainless Steel - Bright

For printing clarity, the lighting environment has been changed to **Empty***. The lighting environment in your software is* **ID Bloom** *and displays differently.*

9. Click **Close** to close the Replace Imported Materials dialog box. Close the Material Properties dialog box. The Materials interface and the vise (with its replaced materials) are shown in Figure 3–57. The Empty environment has been assigned for printing clarity.

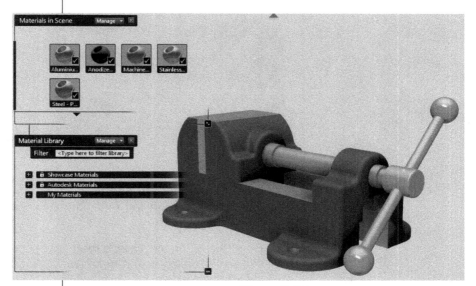

Figure 3–57

Task 2 - Adding an image map.

---

1. In the Material interface, right-click on the Steel-Polished material and select **Duplicate**.

2. A new material swatch is created. Right-click on the new material swatch and select **Rename**.

---

3. Rename the material as **Thread**, as shown in Figure 3–58.

Figure 3–58

4. In the ViewCube, select the **LEFT** label. The vise displays in the Left view.

5. Select the body of the handle subassembly, as shown in Figure 3–59.

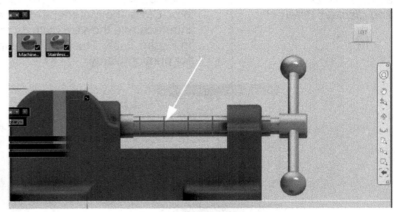

Figure 3–59

6. In the Material interface, right-click on the Thread material and select **Assign to Selection**. Note that a checkmark on the Thread material indicating that it is assigned to an object in the scene.

7. Double-click on the Thread material to open its Material Properties dialog box. Alternatively, you can right-click and select **Properties**.

8. In the dialog box, select **Relief Pattern**. In the Type drop-down list, select **Custom-Image**, as shown in Figure 3–60.

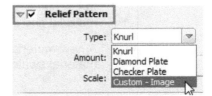

Figure 3–60

9. Next to *Source* field, click 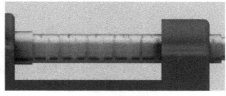 to open the Select File dialog box. Browse to the *Vise_Material* folder of your practice files folder and select **Screw_Threads.jpg**. Click **Open**. The **Screw_Threads.jpg** is listed in the *Source* field and the image displays in the image box, as shown in Figure 3–61. In the viewport, the image displays on the subassembly, as shown in Figure 3–62.

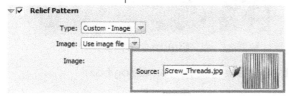

Figure 3–61

Figure 3–62

10. In the *Position* area, set *Rotation* to **1.80**. In *Scale* area, set *Sample Size Width* to **5 cm** (**0'2"**) and *Height* to **30 cm** (**1'0"**). In the *Repeat* area, verify that both *Horizontal* and *Vertical* are set to **Tile**. Set *Amount* to **2.00** and select **Invert Image**, as shown in Figure 3–63.

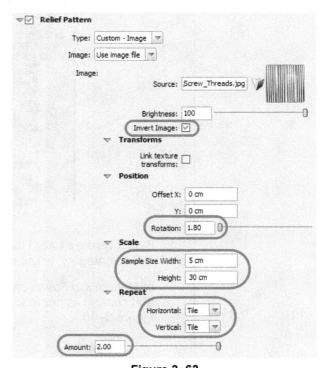

Figure 3–63

- The handle displays with the thread image as shown in Figure 3–64.

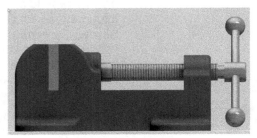

Figure 3–64

11. Close the Material Properties dialog box.

Task 3 - Adding decal map.

1. In the Material interface, in the *Materials Library* category, expand **Showcase Materials>Decals**, as shown in Figure 3–65.

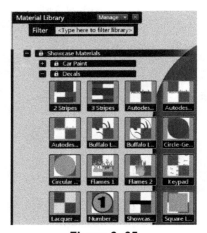

Figure 3–65

2. Select **Square Label** to add its swatch to the *Materials in Scene* category, which displays in alphabetical order.

3. In *Materials in Scene* category, right-click and select **Rename** and change its name to **Ascent Decal**, as shown in Figure 3–66.

Figure 3–66

4. In the viewport, zoom out and pan so that the complete vise displays and the Material interface swatches are not overlapping the vise.

5. Select the base body of the vise, as shown in Figure 3–67.

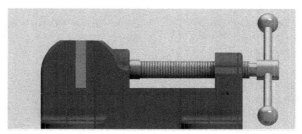

Figure 3–67

6. Verify that the Transform Handles display on the selected geometry. If they are not displayed press <H> to display them.

7. In the *Materials in Scene* category, right-click on Ascent Decal and select **Assign to Selection as Decal**. Note that a yellow star (decal grip) displays on the object and the transform handles are automatically moved on the yellow star. If the decal grip is not clearly displayed and not selected in the Left view, use the **Orbit** navigation tool to locate and select the decal grip. Selecting the grip highlights the object to which it is assigned. In Figure 3–68, the decal grip (star) is shown planar and displayed horizontally.

Based on the current scaling and position of the material you might not be able to currently display the decal grip (star). Once you complete the following steps it will be displayed.

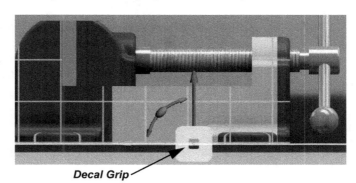

Decal Grip

Figure 3–68

You can toggle the Material interface open/ close by pressing <M> if the swatches are overlapping the object in the viewport.

8. In the *Materials in Scene* category, double-click on the Ascent Decal material or right-click and select **Properties** to open its Material Properties dialog box.

9. Place the dialog box and the model side-by-side so that both are fully displayed.

10. In the dialog box, in the *Decal* area, click 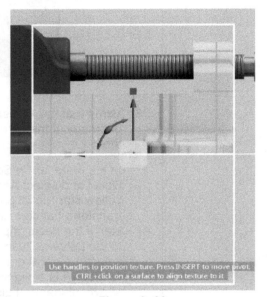 to open the Import File dialog box. Browse to the *Vise_Material* folder of your practice files folder, and select and open **ASCENT.jpg**. The **ASCENT.jpg** image displays in the image box.

*If **Move Texture** is grayed out in the Material Properties dialog box, return to the scene, and locate and select the decal grip.*

11. Click **Move Texture** to display the decal size (white box) along with the transform handles, as shown in Figure 3–69.

Use handles to position texture. Press INSERT to move pivot.
CTRL+click on a surface to align texture to it

Figure 3–69

12. In the Material Properties dialog box, set the *Rotate* values to **90.00**, **-0.00**, and **-90.00**, as shown in Figure 3–70. Note in the viewport how the grip has rotated and is facing in the correct direction and the decal box has moved to the right side of the vise body.

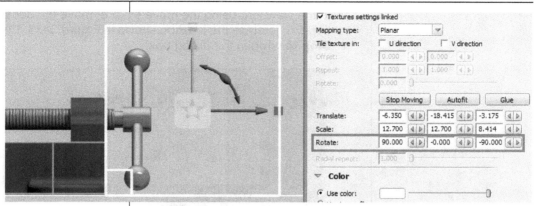

Figure 3–70

*If you deselect the decal grip, click **Move Texture** in the dialog box to select it again.*

13. In the viewport, use the X handle to move the decal map on top of the vise body such that the right box boundary lines up along the right side of the vise body (gray area) as shown in Figure 3–71.

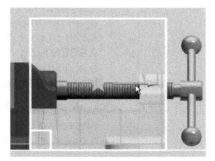

Figure 3–71

14. Set the *Scale* values to **7.000**, **2.000**, and **3.000**, as shown in Figure 3–72. The decal is scaled in the viewport.

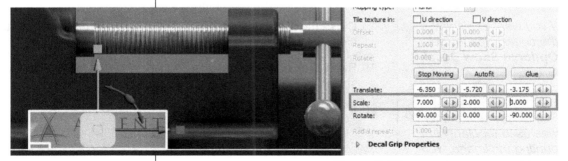

Figure 3–72

---

15. In the viewport, using the move square, move the decal approximately to the location shown in Figure 3–73. Click **Stop Moving** in the dialog box.

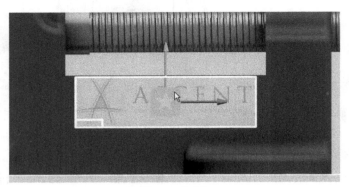

Figure 3–73

16. Using the scroll bar in the dialog box, scroll to the *Transparency* area. Select **Use image file** and click  to open the Import File dialog box. Browse to the *Vise_Material* folder of your practice files folder, and select and open **ASCENT.jpg**. The **ASCENT.jpg** image displays in the image box. In the viewport, the white background of the image is no longer displayed.

17. In the Material Properties dialog box, scroll to the *Color* area and move the **Use color** slider all the way to the left to apply a black color, as shown in Figure 3–74.

Figure 3–74

*If you want to display the decal grips, select **Options>Show Decal Grips**.*

18. Close the Material Properties dialog box and press <Esc> to clear the selection in the viewport.

19. Right-click on the decal grip and select **Hide Decal Grips,** as shown in Figure 3–75.

20. If the Hide Decal Grips dialog box displays, click **OK**.

The Empty environment was used for clarity in printing the image. Your model display will be different.

21. In the ViewCube, click 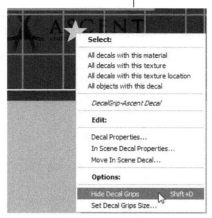 (Home) to orient the model to the default orientation shown in Figure 3–76.

Figure 3–75   **Figure 3–76**

22. Save the file as **MyVise_Material.a3s**.

Practice 3c

Environment Lights and Accent Lights

Practice Objective

- Add and modify the environment lights, shadows, and accent lights in a scene.

Estimated time for completion: 20 minutes

In this practice you will add an environment and modify its lighting and shadows. You will then add an accent light to add brightness to the objects in the scene.

Task 1 - Modifying environment lights and shadows.

1. Click  (Your File) in the (Open File) Task UI or select **File>Open**.

2. In the Open File dialog box, browse to the *Building_Material* folder of your practice files folder. Select and open **Building_Material. a3s**. An exterior of a building, lamp posts, and a parking lot display, as shown in Figure 3–77.

Figure 3–77

3. Select **Appearance>Lighting Environment Library** or press <E> to toggle on the display of the Lighting Environment interface. Note that in the *Environments in Scene* category, **Empty** displays and is currently used in the scene.

4. Expand the **Environment Libraries>Geometry Background>**_Exterior_ category and select the **Grass Field** environment, as shown in Figure 3–78.

Figure 3–78

5. The building is placed in the Grass Field environment. The **Grass Field** environment swatch is added to the _Environments in Scene_ category and surrounded by a blue border, indicating that it is now active.

6. In the _Environments in Scene_ category, right-click on the Grass Field environment and select **Rename.** Change its name to **MyEnvironment**, as shown in Figure 3–79. Press <E> to toggle the Environments interface off.

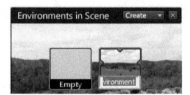

Figure 3–79

7. Select **Appearance>Directional Light and Shadows** to open the Directional Light and Shadows dialog box to control the lighting and shadow properties of the environment. Keep the dialog box open and move it to the side of the screen.

8. In the Navigation Bar, click ⬛ (Zoom Window) and drag a window around the lamp post shown in Figure 3–80.

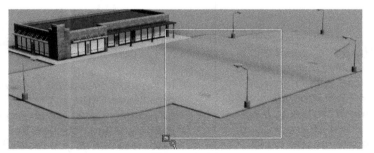

Figure 3–80

9. Release the cursor to zoom into the lamp post, as shown in Figure 3–81. Note how the lamp post shadow is falling on the parking lot surface.

Figure 3–81

10. In the Directional Light and Shadows dialog box, in the *Shadow Properties for All Environments* area, click and drag the Softness slider to the left. Release the mouse and note how the shadow becomes sharper. Move it to **0%**, as shown in Figure 3–82.

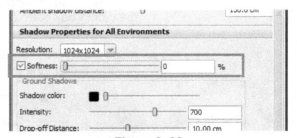

Figure 3–82

The environment name (i.e., MyEnvironment) is added to the name of the Light Properties area in the dialog box to indicate which environment is being modified.

11. In the *Light Properties for MyEnvironment Environment* area, click **Move Light**. In the viewport, near the top in the environment area (as shown in Figure 3–83), click and drag the cursor and note how the position of the shadows change. Also note that as you move the cursor the **Azimuth offset** and **Elevation** values in the dialog box change interactively.

Figure 3–83

12. Click **Stop Moving** and click **Default Position** to restore the original light settings of the environment. In the default position, the light is falling toward the front of the building.

13. In the ViewCube, click 🏠 (Home) to orient the model to its default position.

The azimuth angle moves the light horizontally in the environment dome.

14. To set the light to fall from another direction, set *Azimuth offset* to **160**. Note how the light now falls from the back of the building. The front of the building is darker and the shadows are now falling in the opposite direction, as shown in Figure 3–84.

The elevation value moves the light vertically in the environment dome.

15. To make the shadows longer or shorter, change the Elevation value. Set *Elevation* to **20** and note how the shadows are elongated, as shown in Figure 3–85.

Figure 3–84　　　　　　　　**Figure 3–85**

• Changing the azimuth offset and elevation values enables you to display the scene at different times of the day, in different seasons, and in different geographic locations.

16. Note how the shadows of the parking lot surface are displaying on the ground, as shown on the left in Figure 3–86. In the *Shadow Properties for All Environments* area, in *Ground Shadows* area, set the *Drop-off Rate* to **0.20**, as shown on the right in Figure 3–86. Note how the shadows on the ground become softer.

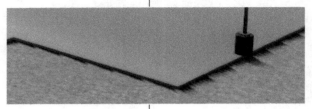 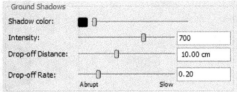

Figure 3–86

17. You can remove the shadows entirely by selecting **All objects** and **Objects** in the two drop-down lists in the *Shadow Casting for All Environments* area, as shown in Figure 3–87.

Figure 3–87

18. Close the Directional Light and Shadows dialog box.

Task 2 - Adding accent lights.

1. In the current environment light's position, the front of the building is dark and visibility is low. Select **Appearance> Accent Lights** or press <L> to open the Accent Lights interface.

2. In the Accent Lights interface, click **Create** and select **Selective Spot Light**, as shown in Figure 3–88.

Figure 3–88

*If the Accent Light's grip is not displayed, select **Options>Show Accent Light Grips**.*

3. The **Spot Light** swatch is added to the Accent Lights interface and the Light grip is placed in the viewport, as shown in Figure 3–89. Right-click on the swatch and select **Rename** and name the accent light as **Building Light** as shown in Figure 3–89.

Figure 3–89

4. Press <O> to open the Organizer and select **Exterior_Architectural_Model.fbx**, as shown on the right in Figure 3–90. The model of the building is selected, as shown on the left.

Figure 3–90

You have to associate objects with an accent light for it to affect the scene.

5. In the Accent Light interface, right-click on the **Building Light** swatch and select **Add Selection To**, as shown in Figure 3–91.

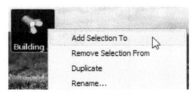

Figure 3–91

*You can also right-click on the Light grip and select **Accent Light Properties** or press <Ctrl>+<L> or double-click on the swatch.*

6. Close the Organizer and press <Esc> to clear the selection.

7. In the Accent Lights interface, right-click on the **Building Light** swatch and select **Properties** to open the Accent Light Properties dialog box.

8. For *Auto placement*, click **Choose>>** and select **In Front of Lit Objects**. For *Light contribution*, select **Environment dependent**, if required as shown in Figure 3–92.

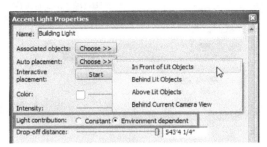

Figure 3–92

9. Note that the front of the building is brighter as shown in Figure 3–93.

Figure 3–93

10. Close the Accent Light Properties dialog box.

11. Save the file as **MyBuilding_Material.a3s**.

Chapter Review Questions

1. Which of the following statements are true regarding the Environments in Scene interface? (Select all that apply.)

   a. The Environments in Scene interface contains a full listing of all of the possible library environments that can be used in the scene.

   b. When a model is imported or opened, the Empty scene is identified in the Environments in Scene interface as the active environment.

   c. All environments listed in the Environments in Scene interface are either currently active or were previously set as an active environment in the scene.

   d. A custom environment can be created using the Environments in Scene interface.

2. Once a model has been imported or opened in a scene you must place the model on the floor. You cannot move the floor location relative to the model.

   a. True

   b. False

3. Which of the following two lighting types is set based on the environment and cannot be changed?

   a. IBL (Image Based Lighting)

   b. Environment Light

4. Which of the following are valid methods of editing lights in a scene? (Select all that apply.)

   a. In the Environments in Scene interface, ensure that the environment is active and drag the cursor anywhere in the viewport to move the light.

   b. In the Task UI, click and drag the cursor anywhere in the viewport to move the light.

   c. In the Task UI, click and drag the cursor anywhere in the viewport to move the light.

   d. Select **Appearance>Directional Light and Shadows** and use the Directional Light and Shadows dialog box.

5. Which of the following are valid accent light types that can be used in a scene?

   a. Ambient Light

   b. Spot Light

   c. Point Light

   d. Directional Light

6. Based on the image shown in Figure 3–94, which of the following two statements is true?

Figure 3–94

   a. A spot light has been added to the scene and transformation handles have been displayed to reposition the light.

   b. A Point light has been added to the scene and transformation handles have been displayed to reposition the light.

7. Which of the following are valid methods of disabling an accent light in a scene?

   a. Select the corresponding accent light's grip and press <H>.

   b. Right-click on the accent light's grip and select **Hide Accent Light Grips**.

   c. Right-click on the accent light's swatch in the Accent Lights interfaces and select **Hide**.

   d. Hide the accent light using the Organizer.

8. Match the following swatches with their descriptions.

a. Indicates that a material texture used in the material cannot be found.

b. Indicates that the material is being used in an alternative but that alternative is not currently displayed in the viewport.

c. Indicates that the material is not currently assigned to any object in the scene.

d. Indicates that the material is currently assigned in the scene.

e. Indicates that the material is linked to the material in the original software in which the object was created.

9. Which of the following commands should be used to assign a material from one object and assign it to another?

   a. **Save to Library**

   b. **Assign to Selection**

   c. **Copy/Paste Material**

   d. **Replace Materials**

10. Which of the following are valid material properties that can be controlled in the Material Properties dialog box to customize material properties? (Select all that apply.)

   a. **Color**

   b. **Lighting**

   c. **Reflectivity**

   d. **Transparency**

   e. **Shadows**

   f. **Bump**

11. Which of the images indicates a Decal grip?

a.

b.

c.

d.

Command Summary

Interface Component	Access Location
Accent Lights	• **Menu Bar:** Appearance>Accent Lights • **Shortcut Key:** <L>
Adjust Lighting (Light and Shadow)	• **Task UI:**
Lighting Environments & Backgrounds	• **Task UI:** • **Menu Bar:** Appearance>Lighting Environment Library • **Shortcut Key:** <E>
Materials	• **Menu Bar:** Appearance>Materials Library • **Shortcut Key:** <M> • **Task UI:** Click (Look)> (Materials)

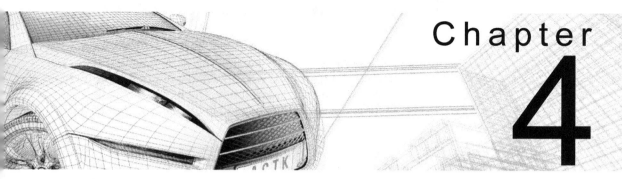

Chapter

4

Presentation Components

In this chapter you learn how to create design alternatives to add variations based on the visibility of items, different materials for parts, and the position of objects in the scene. You learn to create cross-sections to display the inner configurations of objects. You also learn to create still shots of the current camera view of the scene and moving shots to add cinematic movement. You learn to add behaviors to animate the objects in the scene.

Learning Objectives in this Chapter

- Create lineups that enable you to create alternate visibility, material, and positional design configurations.
- Create cross-sections in objects to display their inner configurations.
- Create and control the properties of various types of shots.
- Create a Turntable behavior and a Keyframe Animation behavior

Autodesk Showcase Workflow

Figure 4–1 shows the overall suggested workflow for the Autodesk® Showcase® software. The horizontal line at the top represents the high-level workflow and each of their sub-steps are detailed vertically below them. The highlighted column represents the content discussed in the current chapter.

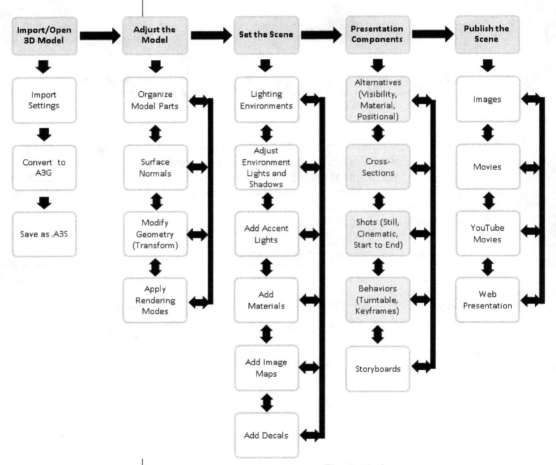

Figure 4–1

4.1 Design Alternatives

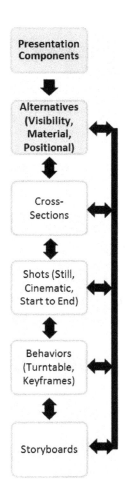

To present your designs effectively, the Autodesk Showcase software enables you to create alternatives or variations of the model and enables you to easily and quickly switch between those visual representations while presenting your design. You might want to set up alternatives to display different parts in a model, display the design with different materials and colors applied to different parts, and different viewing angles to focus on the specific areas of interest.

The alternative variations are created and managed using the Alternative Lineups interface. You can toggle the Alternative Lineups interface open/closed by selecting **Story>Alternatives** or pressing <A>. The Alternative Lineups display to the right of the viewport with all of the created lineups, as shown in Figure 4–2.

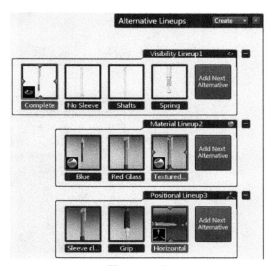

Figure 4–2

Alternative Lineups

You can create three types of alternative lineups, as shown in Figure 4–3. In the Alternative Lineups, click **Create** and select the alternative type that you want to create.

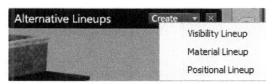

Figure 4–3

- **Visibility Lineup:** Set up alternatives to display different parts in a model by showing/hiding different parts, as shown in Figure 4–4.

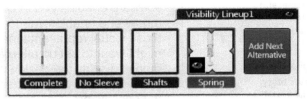

Figure 4–4

- **Material Lineup:** Create material alternatives by assigning different colors and materials to parts of the model, as shown in Figure 4–5.

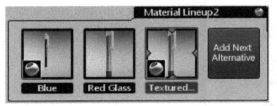

Figure 4–5

- **Positional Lineup:** Create alternatives to display the models at different locations and variations of views, as shown in Figure 4–6.

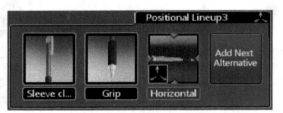

Figure 4–6

Each type of lineup is indicated by a specific icon located in the lineup label.

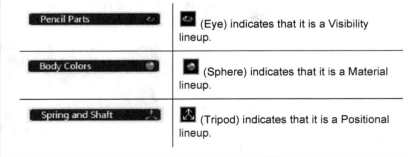

How To: Create Alternatives in a Lineup

1. Open the Alternative Lineups interface by pressing <A> or selecting **Story>Alternatives**.
2. Click **Create** and select the alternative type (**Visibility**, **Material**, or **Positional**) that you want to create. The Lineup is created with a default name. To rename it, right-click on the name type label and select **Rename Lineup** or double-click on the lineup type label and enter a new name to identify its purpose, as shown in Figure 4–7.

Figure 4–7

If you cannot select objects in the viewport, you are in Presentation mode. Press <Tab> to change to Edit mode.

3. In the scene, select the objects for the alternative and click

   . If an alternative is already added to that lineup,

   displays.

   If you do not select objects before selecting **Add Next Alternative**, an **Empty** alternative swatch is created. Select objects in the viewport, right-click on the alternative and select **Add Selection To**.

4. Once an alternative has been created, do the following as required:
   - Right-click on the alternative name and select **Rename Alternative** or double-click to change the name.
   - To add or remove scene objects to an already created alternative, select the objects in the viewport, right-click on the alternative, and select **Add Selection to** or **Remove Selection From**, as shown in Figure 4–8.
   - To easily recognize the alternative from its swatch, set a relevant image in the alternative swatch. Right-click on the alternative and select **Set Image**, as shown in Figure 4–8. A snapshot of the current viewport is set in the alternative swatch.

- Right-click and use the other options for duplicating, deleting, and selecting content, as shown in Figure 4–8.

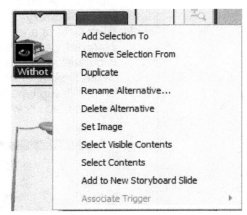

Figure 4–8

Hint: Using Multiple Visibility Lineups

Multiple Visibility Lineups can be used in conjunction with one another to further customize the display. In a situation where you only want one visibility in one of the Lineups to be displayed, consider adding an Empty alternative to the other lineup and activating it, as shown in Figure 4–9.

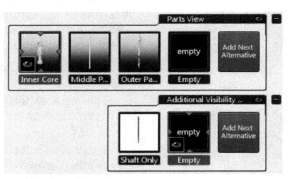

Figure 4–9

4.2 Cross-Sections

Cross-sections are planes that can cut through an object to display the inner configurations of a model. Cross-sectional views can be saved as alternatives and presented as part of your design configuration. You can use a single cross-section plane, as shown on the left in Figure 4–10, or a cross-section corner (three planes forming a corner), as shown on the right in Figure 4–10.

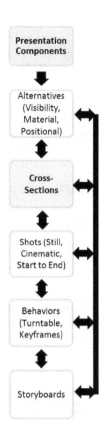

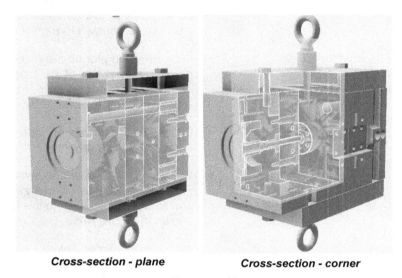

Cross-section - plane   *Cross-section - corner*

Figure 4–10

How To: Create Cross-Sections

1. Open the Cross-Sections interface by pressing <X> or selecting **Appearance>Cross-Sections**. The Cross-Sections interface is shown in Figure 4–11.

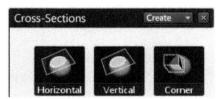

Figure 4–11

2. Select the objects to which the cross-section will be applied.

3. In the Cross-Sections interface, click **Create** and select the cross-section type (**Plane** or **Corner**), as shown in Figure 4–12.

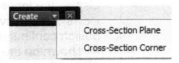

Figure 4–12

4. A cross-section is applied to the selected objects and a corresponding swatch is added to the Cross-Sections interface, as shown in Figure 4–13.

- Cross-section planes are placed at the center of the selected objects. The center of the cross-sectional plane or the corner of the cross-sectional corner coincides with the center of the bounding box of the selected objects.

- Cross-section planes are objects and can be selected and transformed like any other object in the scene.

- You can right-click on the swatch and use options to rename, duplicate, and delete cross-sections. Other options to add and remove objects from the cross-section selection are shown in Figure 4–13.

If no objects are selected, the cross-section is placed at the center of the bounding box of all of the objects in the scene.

Figure 4–13

- Activate a cross-section by selecting the associated swatch in the Cross-Sections interface or in the Organizer, as shown in Figure 4–14.

Figure 4–14

- Once a cross-section has been created it automatically displays in the model. To hide it from the display, click ⬤ next to the cross-section name in the Organizer. Click ⬤ to unhide the cross-section.

- As with other objects, you can use the Transform handles or Transform dialog box, to modify the placement of the cross-section. Select the cross-section and press <H> to display the transform handles. Use the direction arrows, rotation angles, and scale boxes to modify the placement of the cross-section, as shown in Figure 4–15.

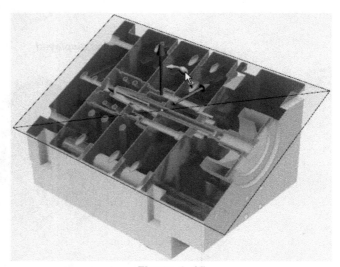

Figure 4–15

Cross-Section Properties

When applied to the objects in the viewport, the cross-section object displays as two parts:

*The display of the cross-section grip can be toggled on/off by selecting **Options> Show Cross-Section Grips** or pressing <Shift>+<X>.*

- **Grip:** The cross-sectional planes used for either a planar cross-section or a corner cross-section are called a *grip*, as shown in Figure 4–16. By default, the grip may be clear and cannot be seen. This is controlled with the Cross-Section Plane properties.

- **Outline:** The lines generated at the point of intersection between the cross-section plane(s) and the selected object are called *Outlines*. The display of outlines can be controlled. In the model shown at the top of Figure 4–16, the outlines display. In the bottom image they have been hidden. This is controlled with the Cross-Section Plane properties.

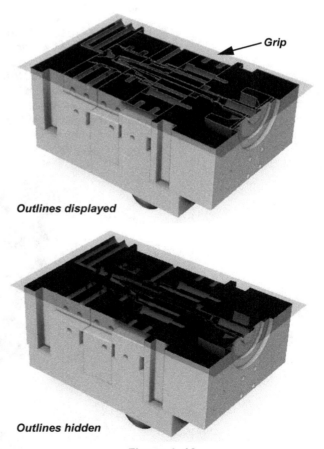

Outlines displayed

Outlines hidden

Figure 4–16

The Cross-Section dialog box (shown in Figure 4–17) can be used to control the properties of a cross-section. To open this dialog box, right-click on the cross-section swatch and select **Properties**, or select **Appearance>Cross-Section Properties**.

*The Cross-Section dialog box titlebar displays the name of the cross-section. In this case, **Horizontal** is the name of the cross-section.*

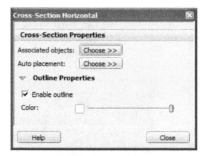

Figure 4–17

The options in the Cross-Section dialog box enable you to control the cross-section and the outline properties, as follows:

Associated objects	Click **Choose** and select from the options. They enable you to add a new object to those currently being cross-sectioned, remove a selected object from those being cross-sectioned, or select the objects that are currently being cross-sectioned.
Auto placement	Click **Choose** and select from the options. They enable you to align the plane along the nearest X-, Y-, or Z-axis if the cross-section is at an angle, center it on the current bounding box center (if you added or removed objects from selection), or flip it by rotating it by 180 degrees.
Enable Outline	Toggles the display of the cross-section's outline lines on or off.
Color	Use the color swatch and slider to set the color of the grip and the associated outline lines.

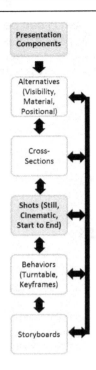

4.3 Shots

Shots are preset views of a scene that can be put together to animate the design. The viewing angle and magnification of objects can be set to focus on an a specific area or object that is to be presented and a view or shot is then saved. Figure 4–18 shows four examples of saved shots. You can also add cinematic movement to the shots to create animated views.

Figure 4–18

How To: Create Shots

1. Select **Story>Camera Shots** or press <T> to access the Shots interface. Alternatively, in the Task UI, click ◖ (Look) to open the Look panel and click 🔲 (Shots). The Shots interface displays as shown in Figure 4–19.

Figure 4–19

2. Manipulate the viewing angle and magnification, as required, to obtain the required view.
3. In the Shots interface, click **Create** and select a Shot type from the list, as shown in Figure 4–20.

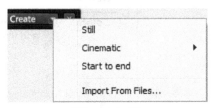

Figure 4–20

It is also possible to create shots outside the Shots interface. Select Story>Create Shot and select the type of shot. This creates a new shot that is added to the Shots interface.

4. A shot of the current viewport is created and displayed as a swatch in the Shots interface. Rename the swatch as required by right-clicking on the name titlebar and selecting **Rename** or by double-clicking on the name titlebar.

Types of Shots

*For **Cinematic** and*

*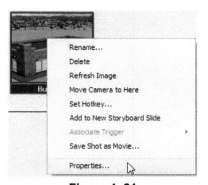 **Start to end** shots,*
*displays in the lower right corner of the **Shots** swatch.*

Three types of shots are available in the Autodesk Showcase software:

Still	Creates a single shot without any motion or magnification of the current view.
Cinematic	Creates a shot with the camera movement along a predefined path. The path is dependent on the selected cinematic type. The type options are shown below.

Still	
Cinematic	▶ Orbit
Start to end	Zoom in
	Zoom out
Import From Files...	Track left
	Track right
	Crane up/left
	Crane up/right

Start to end	Creates a moving shot that moves the view between two keyframes.

Shots Properties

In the Shots interface, when you click **Create** and select the type of shot, the Shot Properties dialog box automatically opens, enabling you to set its properties. To access the properties after the shot has been created, right-click on the **Shots** swatch in the Shot interface and select **Properties**, as shown in Figure 4–21.

Rename...
Delete
Refresh Image
Move Camera to Here
Set Hotkey...
Add to New Storyboard Slide
Associate Trigger ▶
Save Shot as Movie...
Properties...

Figure 4–21

By default, the Motion type listed in the Shot Properties dialog box is set to the shot type that was selected when the Shot was created. You can change it to a different shot type by selecting an option in the Motion type drop-down list.

The Shots Properties dialog box (shown in Figure 4–22), has two areas: *General* and *Camera Motion*. The parameters listed in the *General* area are common for all shot types. The parameters in *Camera Motion* area vary depending on the type of shot selected.

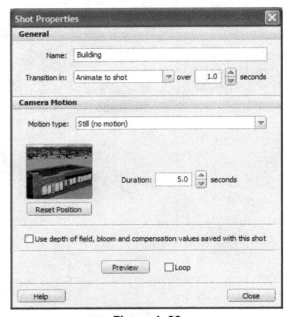

Figure 4–22

General Area

The *General* area for all Shot types is shown in Figure 4–23.

Figure 4–23

Name	Assigns the name of the shot.
Transition	Sets the method to use to transition to the start of the shot. The selected transition is used when the shot is started from the previous shot position.

Transition in: Animate to shot ▼ over 1.0 ▲▼ seconds

Fade from black into shot
Animate to shot
Cut to shot

- **Fade from black into shot:** Starts with a black screen and then displays the shot view. Both the black screen and the camera view display over the time specified in seconds.
- **Animate to shot:** Pans and zooms from the previous shot position to the starting position of this camera view and the whole transition is completed over the time specified in seconds.
- **Cut to shot:** Abruptly moves to the starting position of the shot from the previous shot position and does not have any time associated with it.

Camera Motion Area for Still Shots

The *Camera Motion* area for the Still (no motion) type is shown in Figure 4–24.

Preview and *Loop* are common for all of the Motion types.

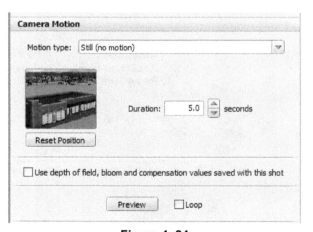

Figure 4–24

Reset Position	Changes the position and magnification of the shot to the current view displayed in the viewport.
Preview	Enables you to preview the shot in the viewport.
Use depth of field, bloom and compensation values saved with this shot	Playback will use the depth of field, bloom, and compensation settings saved with the shot.
Loop	Plays the shot continually from the beginning until you select a different shot to play.

Camera Motion Area for Cinematic Shots

The *Camera Motion* area for the Cinematic (one keyframe plus path) type is shown in Figure 4–25.

*If you select **Orbit** in the Motion Path drop-down list, the setting options are different.*

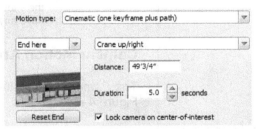

Figure 4–25

Reset Start/ Reset Half-way/ Reset Find	Adds the path of movement at the starting position, half-way position, or end position based on the position selected in the drop-down list.
Motion Path	Enables you to select the path of the motion.
Distance and Duration	Sets the distance and time to play the animation.
Lock camera on center-of-interest	The starting point, halfway point, or ending point is set to the center of interest of the scene.

Camera Motion Area for Start to End Shots

The *Camera Motion* area for the Start to end (two keyframes) type is shown in Figure 4–26.

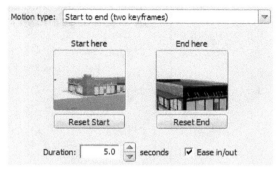

Figure 4–26

Reset Start/ Reset End	Sets the position and magnification of the first keyframe and the second (ending) keyframe.
Duration	Sets the time to play the animation.
Ease in/out	Controls whether the starting and ending motions are slowed down as they are being approached or if they are approached more abruptly.

Hint: Assigning Hotkeys to Shots

Assigning hotkeys to shots can be useful while presenting. The hotkeys play the shots outside the Shots interface. In the Shots interface, right-click on a **Shot** swatch and select **Set Hotkey** to open the Hotkey Editor, as shown on the left in Figure 4–27. Expand the Key drop-down list and select the hotkey number. The hotkey is assigned to the shot and displays on the upper right side of the **Shot** swatch, as shown on the right in Figure 4–27.

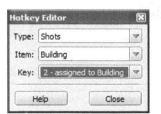 

Figure 4–27

Hint: Creating Shots while Importing/Opening

When importing or opening a 3D file, predefined standard shots can be created using the Import Settings dialog box. In the Import Settings dialog box, in the *3D Model* tab, in the *Shot* area, select the checkbox and then select the standard shots to be created, as shown in Figure 4–28.

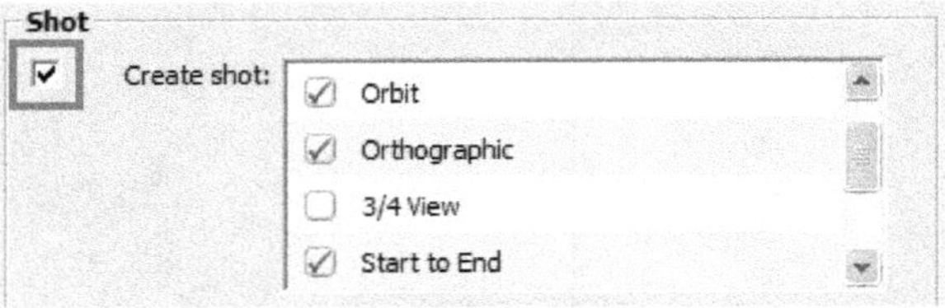

Shot		
☑	Create shot:	☑ Orbit
		☑ Orthographic
		☐ 3/4 View
		☑ Start to End

Figure 4–28

Playing Shots

You can play or view the shots in many different ways.

- You can play each shot individually by clicking on the required swatch in the Shots interface.

- If you have hotkeys that are assigned to shots, you can press the required key to play each shot individually without accessing the Shots interface.

- You can also play all of the created shots sequentially using the Play control buttons in the Shots interface titlebar, as shown in Figure 4–29.

Figure 4–29

4.4 Behaviors

Behaviors are functions that are applied to objects to control their movement and add animation. You can create behaviors in the Behaviors interface, as shown in Figure 4–30.

Figure 4–30

Two types of behaviors can be created: Turntable and Keyframe Animation.

Turntable

A Turntable behavior generates movement rotationally around the floor origin. When a Turntable behavior is created, the pivot location is identified on the model, as shown in Figure 4–31.

Turntable Pivot

Figure 4–31

As an alternative to the rotational movement around the floor origin, you can change the orientation of the pivot so that it rotates around a plane perpendicular to the floor. This rotation is set using the **Rotisserie** option in the Turntable Properties dialog box. Its pivot is shown in Figure 4–32.

Rotisserie Pivot

Figure 4–32

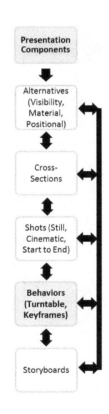

Presentation Components

↓

Alternatives (Visibility, Material, Positional)

↕

Cross-Sections

↕

Shots (Still, Cinematic, Start to End)

↕

Behaviors (Turntable, Keyframes)

↕

Storyboards

The selection of the pivot orientation is usually dependent on the model geometry and the required movement.

How To: Create and Play Turntable Behavior

1. Open the Behaviors interface by pressing <B> or selecting **Story>Behaviors**.
2. Select the objects to which you want to add the behaviors.
3. In the Behaviors interface, click **Create** and select **Turntable**, as shown in Figure 4–33.

You have to associate an object(s) in the scene with a behavior.

Figure 4–33

4. The **Turntable** swatch is added to the Behaviors interface and the Turntable Properties dialog box opens, as shown in Figure 4–34.

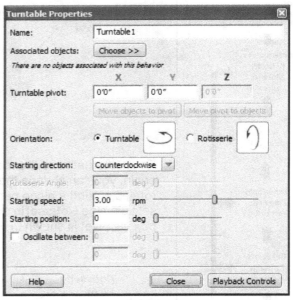

Figure 4–34

Use the parameters in the Turntable Properties dialog box to select the objects to be moved and to modify the settings to obtain the required movement.

Associated objects	Click **Choose>>** to access the options for adding or removing selected geometry to the behavior or for selecting and highlighting the objects in the active behavior.
Turntable pivot	Enables you to enter the X,Y,Z values to move the pivot position. You can also use **Move objects to pivot**, or **Move pivot to objects**, or drag the pivot marker in the viewport to automatically modify the location of the pivot.
Orientation	Enables you to control the movement of objects in either horizontal (**Turntable**) or vertical (**Rotisserie**) motion.
Starting direction, Starting speed, Starting position	Sets the turntable direction (clockwise or counter-clockwise), speed, and position on the pivot from which to start the turntable motion.
Oscillate between	Enables you to set the angles for adding movement.

5. Click **Playback Controls** to open the playing controls, as shown in Figure 4–35. Use the buttons and scroll bar to play, rewind to the beginning, fast forward to end, or drag to a specific point of the animation.

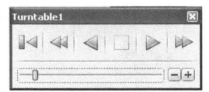

Figure 4–35

- In the Behaviors interface, you can right-click on the **Turntable** swatch and use **Rename**, **Duplicate**, and **Delete**, options to add and remove objects from the turntable selection. Right-click and select **Turntable Controls** to open the controls for playing the turntable.

Keyframe Animation

The Keyframe Animation behavior enables you to create a custom animation by establishing a timeline and defining specific transforms of the model at specific points (or keyframes) on the timeline. Transformations can include changing the position of the model in a plane (pan), rotating it (orbit), or scaling it (zoom). When the timeline is played, movement is established between each keyframe.

How To: Create and Play Keyframe Animation

1. Open the Behaviors interface by pressing <B> or selecting **Story>Behaviors**.
2. Select the objects to which you want to add animation and set the position of the objects at the required location.
3. In the Behaviors interface, click **Create** and select **Keyframe Animation**, as shown in Figure 4–36.

Figure 4–36

4. A **Keyframe** swatch is added to the Behaviors interface and the Keyframe dialog box opens, as shown in Figure 4–37.

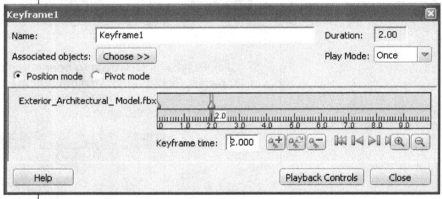

Figure 4–37

Choose>> also enables you to remove a selected object from the behavior and to select and highlight the objects that are associated with the behavior.

5. Click **Choose>>** and select **Add Selection** to assign the selected objects to the keyframe behavior, if not already assigned.
6. In the Keyframe dialog box, select the Timeline at the point at which you want to set the keyframe. Note that a gray bar is added at that location.
7. Click [icon] and note that a tooltip is added to the gray bar, as shown in Figure 4–38. If you need to reposition this keyframe, enter a value in the *Keyframe time* edit box.

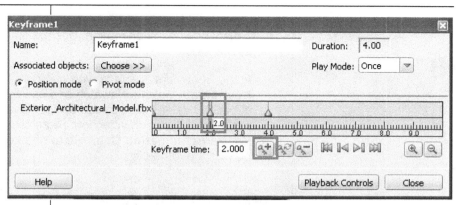

Figure 4–38

- The current location, position, and transformation of the objects are saved at this current keyframe.

8. In the viewport, using the Transform handles and position the objects for the next keyframe.

An orange tooltip on the keyframe bar indicates which keyframe is active on the timeline.

9. Click 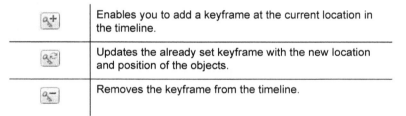. Another keyframe is automatically added at an increment of 1 second. Drag this keyframe to the required point on the timeline or enter a specific value in the *Keyframe time* edit box. Additional keyframe options include the following:

⊕+	Enables you to add a keyframe at the current location in the timeline.
⊕↻	Updates the already set keyframe with the new location and position of the objects.
⊕−	Removes the keyframe from the timeline.

10. Define any of following options, as required.

Position mode	Enables you to set the position of the objects in the viewport at the selected keyframe location in the timeline. Use the transformation tools to set the position and magnification of the selected objects.
Duration	Sets the total duration of the animation.
Play Mode	Sets how you want to play the animation. You can play the it once, in a loop, or oscillating between the start and end of the animation.
▐◀◀ ◀◀ ▶▶ ▶▶▐	Move to the specific keyframes by moving to the first keyframe, previous keyframe, next keyframe, and last keyframe respectively.

11. Click **Playback Controls** to open the playing controls to play, pause, or stop the animation. Use the other playback controls as required.

- In the Behaviors interface, you can right-click on the **Keyframe Animation** swatch and use options to rename, duplicate, delete, etc., to add and remove objects from the Keyframe Animation selection. Right-click and select **KeyframeAnimation Controls** to open the controls for playing the turntable.

Hint: Autodesk Inventor Constraints

Autodesk Inventor assembly constraints can be converted into Autodesk Showcase behaviors when an Autodesk Inventor assembly file is being imported. Select **Create behaviors from constraints** and enter the *Constraint name* in the *Animation* area in the Import Settings dialog box, as shown in Figure 4–39.

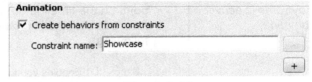

Figure 4–39

Practice 4a

Estimated time for completion: 45 minutes

You can create shots during import to suit your needs and then modify or delete them in the Shots interface.

Alternatives and Shots

Practice Objectives

- Create visibility and material lineup alternatives for objects in a scene.
- Create still and cinematic moving shots.

In this practice you will create visibility lineups for a mechanical pencil, and then add material lineups to the visible objects. You will also create different shots of the current camera position in the scene, add cinematic movements to create moving shots, and play them.

Task 1 - Creating visibility alternative lineups.

1. Click 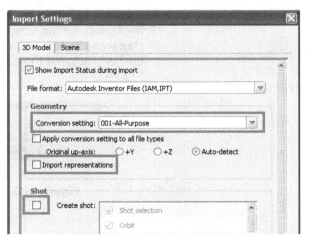 (Your File) in the (Open File) Task UI or select **File>Open**.

2. In the Open File dialog box, browse to the *Pencil_Alternative* folder of your practice files folder.

3. Select **Mechanical Pencil.iam**. Do not open the file.

4. In the Open File dialog box, click **Settings...** to open the Import Settings dialog box. In the *3D Model* tab, verify that *Conversion setting* is set to **001-All Purpose**, and clear the **Import representations** option if required. In the *Shot* area, clear the **Create shot** checkbox to ensure that no default shots are created. Set the options as shown in Figure 4–40.

Figure 4–40

5. Close the Import Settings dialog box and open the file **Mechanical Pencil.iam**.

6. In the Inventor Assembly Settings dialog box, click **Continue** to load the file. After conversion is complete, a 3D model of a mechanical pencil displays, as shown in Figure 4–41.

Figure 4–41

7. Close the Import Status dialog box.

8. Select **Story>Alternatives** or press <A> to toggle on the display of the Alternative Lineups interface.

9. In the Alternative Lineups interface, click **Create** and select **Visibility Lineup**. Note that the Visibility Lineup1 title is created, as shown in Figure 4–42.

10. Right-click on the Visibility Lineup1 titlebar and select **Rename Lineup** or double-click on the Visibility Lineup1 titlebar. Rename the title as **Parts View**, as shown in Figure 4–43.

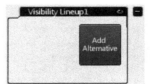

Figure 4–42   **Figure 4–43**

 (Eye) displayed in the Lineup title bar indicates that it is a Visibility lineup.

Hold <Ctrl> to select multiple objects.

11. Open the Organizer by pressing <O> or selecting **Edit> Organizer**.

12. In the Organizer, expand **Mechanical Pencil.iam**. Select **Coupling:1**, **Dispenser Ring:1**, **Dispenser:1**, and **Spring:1** as shown in Figure 4–44.

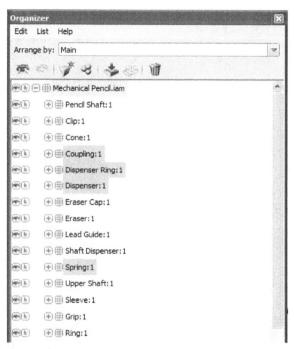

Figure 4–44

If the items are selected before the alternative is created, the items are automatically added to the alternative.

13. In the Alternative Lineups interface, in the Parts View lineup, select **Add Alternative**. A visibility alternative named *Alternate1* is created, as shown on the left in Figure 4–45.

14. Right-click on Alternate1 and select **Rename Alternative** or double-click on the Alternate1 title and rename it as **Inner Core**, as shown on the right in Figure 4–45.

 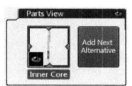

Figure 4–45

15. In the Organizer, select **Pencil Shaft:1**, **Eraser:1**, and **Shaft Dispenser:1**, as shown in Figure 4–46.

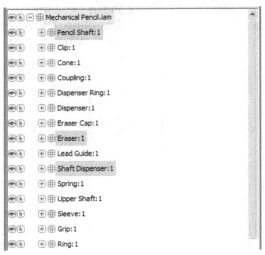

Figure 4–46

16. In the Alternative Lineups interface, in the Parts View lineup, select **Add Next Alternative**. A visibility alternative named *Alternate2* is created. Rename *Alternate2* as **Middle Parts**.

If you select objects that have been included in other alternatives, a warning displays prompting you that some hidden objects are selected.

17. In the Organizer, select the remaining objects as shown on the left in Figure 4–47.

18. In the Alternative Lineups interface, in the Parts View lineup, select **Add Next Alternative**. A visibility alternative named *Alternate3* is created. Rename *Alternate3* as **Outer Parts,** as shown on the right in Figure 4–47.

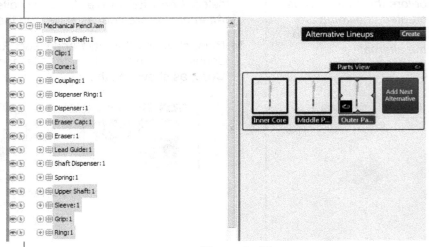

Figure 4–47

19. Close the Organizer.

20. In the Alternative Lineups interface, select the **Inner Core** swatch. Note that only the items included in this alternative display in the viewport.

If the Task UI bar interferes with selecting and viewing objects,

click  *and clear the* **Show Task UI** *option to remove the Task UI from the viewport. To return the Task UI to the display, select **Options> Show Task UI**.*

21. Using  (Zoom Window), in the viewport, drag a window around the visible parts, as shown in Figure 4–48. The objects are zoomed into the viewport.

Figure 4–48

22. In the Alternative Lineups interface, right-click on the **Inner Core** swatch, and select **Set Image**, as shown on the left in Figure 4–49. The new image is set as the image for the **Inner Core** swatch, as shown on the right in Figure 4–49.

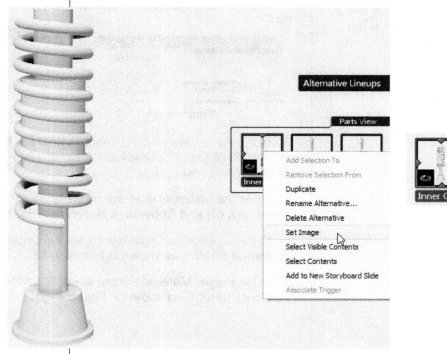

Figure 4–49

In the viewport, only items that are included in the active visibility alternative display.

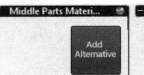 *(Sphere) displayed in the Lineup title bar indicates that it is a Materials lineup.*

23. In the Alternative Lineups interface, select the **Middle Parts** swatch. Use 🔍 (Zoom Fit All) to fill the viewport with the visible objects.

24. Right-click on the **Middle Parts** swatch and select **Set Image**. The new image is set as the image for the **Middle Parts** swatch. Note that all of the images are set, as shown in Figure 4–50.

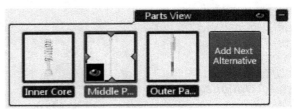

Figure 4–50

Task 2 - Creating material alternative lineups.

1. In the Alternative Lineups interface, click **Create** and select **Material Lineup** as shown in Figure 4–51.

2. Note that Material Lineup2 has been created. Rename it as **Middle Parts Materials**, as shown in Figure 4–52.

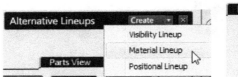

Figure 4–51   **Figure 4–52**

3. In the Parts View visibility lineup, select the **Middle Parts** swatch (if it is not already active) to activate it, so that only the middle part objects display.

4. Open the Materials interface by pressing <M>. In the Material Library, expand **Showcase Materials>Plastic**.

5. In the viewport or Organizer (open the Organizer), select **Pencil Shaft:1** as shown in Figure 4–53.

6. In the Plastic Material Library, select **Blue Matte** to apply it to Pencil Shaft:1, as shown in Figure 4–53.

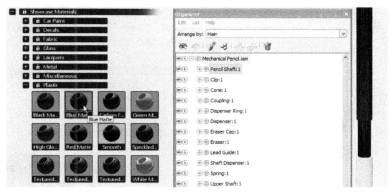

Figure 4–53

7. In the Alternative Lineups interface, in the Middle Parts Materials lineup, select **Add Alternative**. A material alternative named *Alternate1* is created. Rename it as **Blue Shaft**, as shown in Figure 4–54.

8. With **Pencil Shaft:1** still selected, apply **Red Matte** from the Plastic Material Library.

9. In the Alternative Lineups interface, in the Middle Parts Materials lineup, select **Add Next Alternative**. A material alternative named *Alternate2* is created. Rename it as **Red Shaft**, as shown in Figure 4–54.

10. Press <Esc> to clear the selection.

11. Create another Material Lineup for the outer parts of the mechanical pencil. In the Alternative Lineups interface, click **Create** and select **Material Lineup.** A new material lineup is created. Rename it as **Outer Parts Materials**, as shown in Figure 4–55.

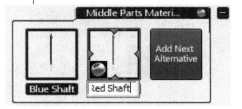

Figure 4–54

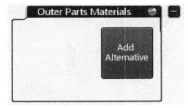

Figure 4–55

12. In the Parts View visibility lineup, select the **Outer Parts** swatch to activate it.

13. In the Organizer, select **Cone:1**, **Eraser Cap:1**, **Upper Shaft:1**, and **Lead Guide:1**, as shown in Figure 4–56.

14. In the Materials interface, in the Material Library, open **Showcase Materials>Metal**. Select **Chrome** to apply it to selected items, as shown in Figure 4–56.

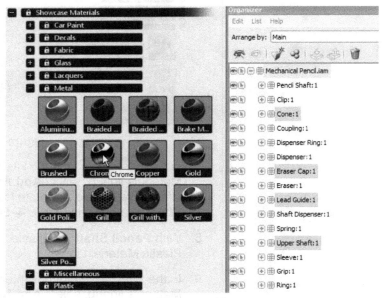

Figure 4–56

15. In the Organizer, select **Clip:1**, **Sleeve:1**, and **Ring:1**. Apply **Blue Metallic** from **Showcase Materials>Lacquers** to the selected items, as shown in Figure 4–57.

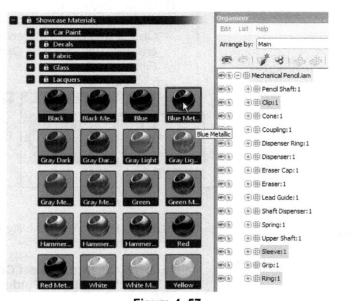

Figure 4–57

16. In the Alternative Lineups interface, in the Outer Parts Materials lineup, select **Add Alternative**. Rename the new alternative as **Blue Lacquer**, as shown in Figure 4–58.

17. With **Clip:1**, **Sleeve:1**, and **Ring:1** still selected, apply **Hammer Red** from **Showcase Materials>Lacquers**.

18. In the Alternative Lineups interface, in the Outer Parts Materials lineup, select **Add Next Alternative**. Rename the new alternative as **Hammer Red**, as shown in Figure 4–58.

19. With **Clip:1**, **Sleeve:1**, and **Ring:1** still selected, apply **Yellow** from the *Lacquers* category and create a material alternative called **Yellow**, as shown in Figure 4–58.

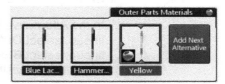

Figure 4–58

20. The complete lineup is shown in Figure 4–59. Save your scene as **mypencil_alternatives.a3s** in the *Pencil_Alternative* folder of your practice files folder.

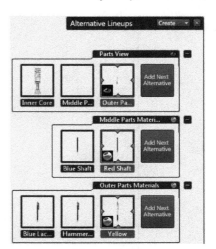

Figure 4–59

21. Close the Materials interface and the Organizer.

22. Clear any selection, if required.

23. Select the **Middle Parts** visibility alternative (Parts View) and select the **Blue Shaft** and **Red Shaft** Middle Parts Materials material alternatives. Note the display for each shaft alternative in the viewport.

24. Select the **Outer Parts** visibility alternative and use the three **Outer Parts Materials** alternatives with it. Note the display in the viewport.

Task 3 - Creating Shots.

If you want default shots to be created on import, select the required shots in the Import Settings dialog box.

1. Select **Story>Camera Shots** or press <T> to open the Shots interface. No shots are available in the interface because the **Shot** option was cleared in the Import Settings dialog box.

2. In the Alternative Lineups interface, in the *Parts View* visibility lineup, select **Outer Parts**. In the *Outer Parts Materials* lineup, select **Blue Lacquer**. Press <F> to fill the viewport with all of the visible objects.

Note that the colors might look different on your screen depending on the reflections.

3. Hold <Alt> and position the pencil at a slant as shown in Figure 4–60.

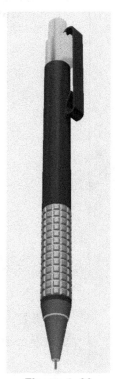

Figure 4–60

4. In the Shots interface, click **Create** and select **Still,** as shown in Figure 4–61. A swatch of the current viewport is created and the Shot Properties dialog box opens.

Figure 4–61

5. In the Shot Properties dialog box, set the name as **Still Image** and set the settings as shown in Figure 4–62. In the *Camera Motion* area, note how the object's image displays. In the viewport, pan and zoom the pencil to reposition it. In the dialog box, click **Reset Position**. The image should display similar to that shown in Figure 4–62. Close the dialog box.

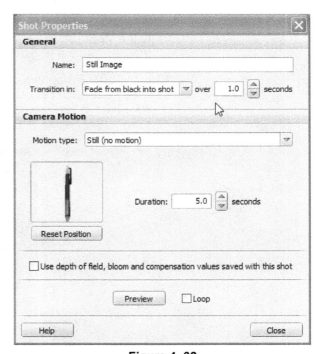

Figure 4–62

6. In the Shots interface, click **Create**, and select **Cinematic> Track left**, as shown in Figure 4–63.

Figure 4–63

7. In the Shot Properties dialog box, set the *Name* to **Cinematic**. Set *Transition in* to **Animate to shot** and set *over* to **1.0** seconds. Select **Loop**, as shown in Figure 4–64, and click **Preview**. Note the motion preview in the viewport. Do not close the dialog box.

8. Click **Stop Preview**.

9. In the viewport, in the ViewCube, click 🏠 (Home) to orient the pencil to the original viewing position.

10. In the Shot Properties dialog box, in the *Camera Motion* area, click **Reset Start** to reset the starting position to the one displayed in the viewport. Select **Crane up/left** and select **Loop**, as shown in Figure 4–65.

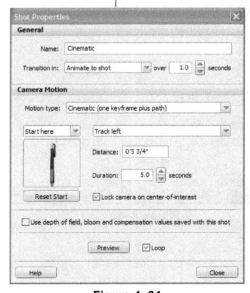

Figure 4–64

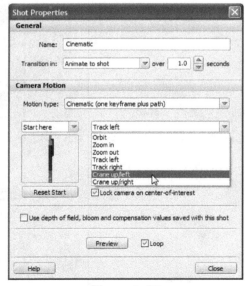

Figure 4–65

11. Click **Preview**. Note the motion of the pencil in the viewport. Click **Stop Preview**.

12. In the *General* area, set *over* to **2.0** seconds to increase the transition. Clear **Loop** and close the dialog box.

13. In the Shots interface, click **Create** and select **Start to end**.

14. In the Shot Properties dialog box, set the name to **Start-end**. Select **Loop**, as shown in Figure 4–66, and click **Preview**. Note the movement in the viewport and click **Stop Preview**.

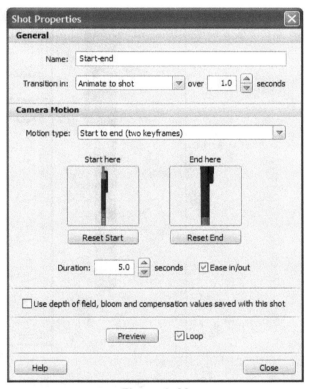

Figure 4–66

15. In the Navigation Bar, click 🔍 (Zoom Window). In the viewport, create a window around the pencil grip and the lead guide, as shown on the left in Figure 4–67.

16. In the dialog box, in the *Camera Motion* area, for *Start here*, click **Reset Start**. In the ViewCube, click 🏠 (Home) and for *End here*, click **Reset End** in the dialog box. In the *General* area, set (*Transition in*) *over* to **5.0 seconds**, as shown on the right in Figure 4–67.

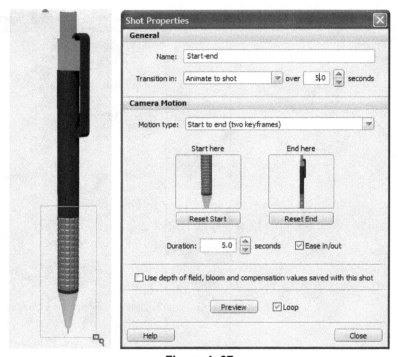

Figure 4–67

17. Select **Loop** and click **Preview**. Note the movement in the viewport and click **Stop Preview**. Clear **Loop** and close the dialog box.

18. In the Shots interface, click **Create** and select **Cinematic> Orbit**.

19. In the ViewCube, click 🏠 (Home).

20. In the Shot Properties dialog box, set the *Name* to **Orbit**. Click **Reset Start** and set *Duration* to **10.0** seconds. Select **Loop**, as shown in Figure 4–68.

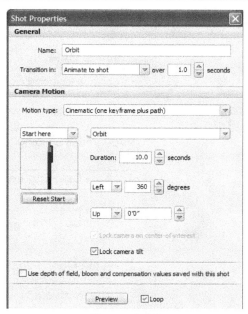

Figure 4–68

21. Click **Preview**. Note the movement in the viewport and click **Stop Preview**. Clear **Loop** and close the dialog box.

22. The Shots Interface displays with all of the shots created, as shown in Figure 4–69. Select each shot to display it in the viewport.

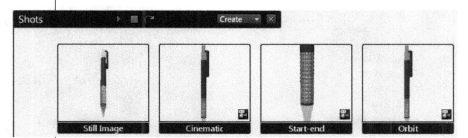

Figure 4–69

23. In the Shots interface title bar, click ▶ (Play all shots) to sequentially play the created shots once. Click ↻ (Loop playback) to play all of the shots sequentially repeatedly. Click ❚❚ to pause or click ■ to stop.

24. Save your scene as **mypencil_shots.a3s** in the *Pencil_Alternative* folder of your practice files folder.

Practice 4b

Estimated time for completion: 30 minutes

If the selection is not clearly visible in the viewport, use the animated grid selection style and note the blue grid lines moving over the door.

Behaviors

Practice Objective

- Create a keyframe animation and add a cross-section.

In this practice you will create a keyframe animation to open and close a door. You will also add a cross-sectional plane that cuts through the building to display the inner layout.

Task 1 - Creating keyframe animation.

1. Click  (Your File) in the (Open File) Task UI or select **File>Open**.

2. In the Open File dialog box, browse to the *Building_ Alternative* folder of your practice files folder. Open **Building_ Alternative.a3s**.

3. Press <O> to open the Organizer. Expand **Exterior_ Architectural_Model.fbx>Outer Doors** and select **AecDbDoor_7800**, as shown on the left in Figure 4–70. Note that in the viewport, the front door of the building is selected, as shown on the right in Figure 4–70. The Transform handles might or might not display depending on whether they are toggled on/off.

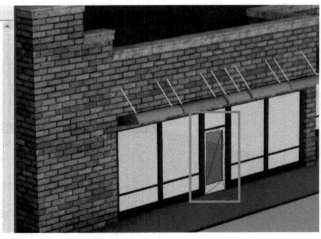

Figure 4–70

4. Right-click in the environment to activate the window and press <F> to fill the screen with the selected door.

5. In the Organizer, select **Windows** and click 👁 as shown on the left in Figure 4–71. The windows are hidden in the viewport. In the Organizer, **Windows** displays in gray and in italics, as shown on the right in Figure 4–71.

You might be required to click on the door first and then press <H> for the transform handles to display.

If your Task UI bar interferes with selecting and viewing the objects,

click 🔵 and select **Show Task UI** *in the menu to clear the option. This removes the Task UI from the viewport.*

Figure 4–71

6. In the Organizer, select **AecDbDoor_7800** again.

7. Press <H> to display the Transform handles, if not already displayed.

8. Press <Insert> to change the transform handles to display the pivot point as shown in Figure 4–72.

9. Hold <S> and select the left edge of the door facing you (anywhere along the vertical edge), as shown in Figure 4–73. Release <S> and press <Insert> again to return to the transform handles and complete the pivot point movement.

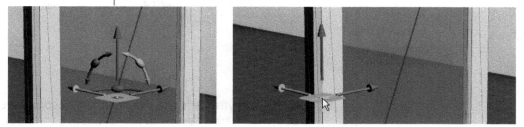

Figure 4–72   **Figure 4–73**

10. In the Organizer, click ⬭ for **Windows** to unhide the window objects, as shown in Figure 4–74.

Figure 4–74

11. Verify that the **AecDbDoor_7800** is still selected.

12. Press <B> or select **Story>Behaviors** to open the Behaviors interface.

13. In the Behaviors interface, click **Create** and select **Keyframe Animation**, as shown in Figure 4–75.

Figure 4–75

If the objects have already been selected, they are automatically associated with the keyframe.

14. The **Keyframe1** swatch displays in the interface, as shown in Figure 4–76. The Keyframe dialog box also opens. Verify that **AecDbDoor_7800** displays with the keyframe bar in the dialog box and also note in the Organizer, a keyframe icon displays along with the selected door. In the dialog box, set the *Name* to **Door**, as shown in Figure 4–76.

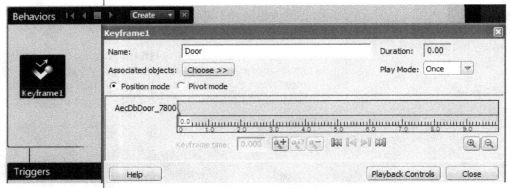

Figure 4–76

15. Note that a keyframe is already set at **0.0** seconds. Select the tip of the keyframe marker to make it active (orange), as shown in Figure 4–77. This saves the original position of the door as a keyframe in the Timeline.

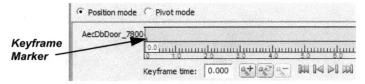

Figure 4–77

16. In the viewport, on the transform handles, select the X-axis Rotation arc (blue) to open the edit box, type **30.0**, as shown in Figure 4–78 and press <Enter>. The door is rotated at the pivot point at an angle of 30 degrees, as shown in Figure 4–78.

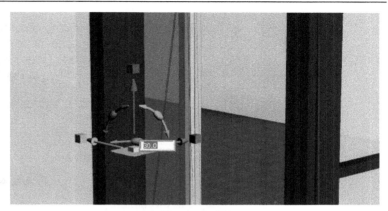

Figure 4–78

17. In the Door (Keyframe) dialog box, click 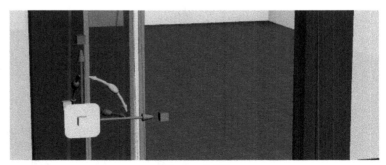 to save this door location as a keyframe. Note that a keyframe is automatically added at **1.0** second (1 second interval). To move the keyframe to the 2.0 seconds location, hold and drag the keyframe marker to **2.0** or type **2.000** in *Keyframe time* edit box and press <Enter>. The dialog box should display as shown in Figure 4–79.

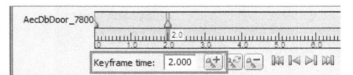

Figure 4–79

18. In the viewport, in the transform tandles, select the X-axis Rotation arc (blue) again to open the edit box. Type **30.0** and press <Enter>. The door is rotated another 30 degrees. Hold <Alt> and drag the cursor to change the viewing angle so that the open door location is visible, as shown in Figure 4–80.

Figure 4–80

19. In the Keyframes dialog box, click 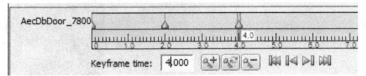 to save the new location as a keyframe. Note that a keyframe is automatically added at **3.0** seconds (1 second interval). Set this *Keyframe time* to **4.000**, as shown in Figure 4–81.

Figure 4–81

20. In the viewport, in the transform handles, select the X-axis Rotation arc (blue) again to open the edit box. Type **-30.0** and press <Enter>. The door is rotated a negative 30 degrees and begins closing.

21. In the Keyframe dialog box, click 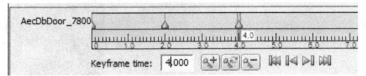 to save the new location as a keyframe. Note that a keyframe is automatically added at **5.0** seconds (1 second interval). Set the *Keyframe time* to **6.000**.

22. In the Keyframe dialog box, set *Play Mode* to **Loop**. Click **Playback Controls** to open the Door playbacks, as shown in Figure 4–82. Click ▷ to play the animation.

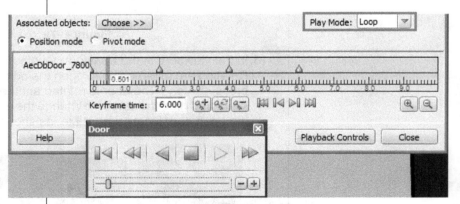

Figure 4–82

- Note that the door opens and closes continuously as it plays in a loop.
- The movement between the closing of the door from the 30 degree angle to the completely closed position is abrupt. You can add another keyframe for the closing position.

If the door is not selected, use the Organizer to select the door.

*You can open the playback controls from the Behavior interface by right-clicking on the **Door** swatch and selecting **KeyframeAnimation controls**.*

23. In the Door playbacks, click [image] to stop the animation. In the Keyframe dialog box, select the **6.0** tooltip to activate it.

24. In the viewport, on the transform handles, select the X-axis Rotation arc (blue) again to open the edit box. Type **-30.0** and press <Enter>.

25. In the Keyframe dialog box, click [image] to save the new location as a keyframe. Note that a keyframe is automatically added at **7.0** seconds (1 second interval). Set the *Keyframe time* to **8.000**.

26. Close the Keyframe dialog box. In the Door playbacks, click

   [image] to play the animation. Note how the door opens and closes.

27. Click [image] to stop the animation and click [image] to move to the reset position.

28. Close all of the dialog boxes and the Behaviors interface.

29. Press <Esc> to clear the selection.

Task 2 - Adding a cross-section.

---

1. Open the Organizer, if required, and select **Exterior_ Architectural_Model.fbx**.

2. In the Navigation Bar, click [image] (Zoom Selected) and close the Organizer. Note that complete building is selected.

3. Select **Appearance>Cross-Sections** or press <X> to open the Cross-Sections interface.

4. In the Cross-Sections interface, click **Create** and select **Cross-Section Plane**, as shown in Figure 4–83.

Figure 4–83

The Empty environment was used for clarity in printing the image. Your model display will be different.

5. The **Plane** swatch is added to the Cross-Sections interface and a cross-section plane is added to the building, as shown in Figure 4–84. The Transform handles might or might not display depending on whether they are toggled on/off. Also your selection display might be different.

Figure 4–84

6. Press <H> to display the Transform Handles, if not already displayed.

7. Hold and drag the Z-axis (blue) of the handles and move the cross-section down until the inner layout of the building displays, as shown in Figure 4–85.

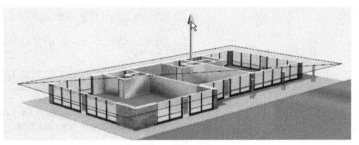

Figure 4–85

8. The cross-section behaves like any other object. Open the Organizer and compress the **Exterior_Architectural_ Model.fbx** object. Note that the **Plane** displays as shown in Figure 4–86.

Figure 4–86

9. Click next to **Plane** to hide the cross-section plane and display the complete building.

10. If you need to present the layout of the building, unhide the cross-section plane by clicking next to **Plane**.

11. Hide the plane and save your scene as **MyBuilding_Alternative.a3s** in the *Building_Alternative* folder of your practice files folder.

Chapter Review Questions

1. Fill in the blanks with the Alternative Lineup types that match the icons that display in their associated Alternative Lineup titlebars. (Hint: The available types include: **Visibility**, **Material**, and **Positional Lineups**.)

    a. (Sphere) ____

    b. (Tripod) ____

    c. (Eye) ____

2. Which of the following statements is true regarding creating a new Visibility alternative if no objects are selected in the viewport?

    a. If no objects are selected, you are prompted to select them so that the alternative can be created.

    b. If no objects are selected, an Empty alternative swatch is added to the lineup.

    c. If no objects are selected, the new alternative is created as a copy of the currently active alternative.

    d. Objects must be selected to create a Visibility Lineup. If no objects are selected an alternative cannot be created.

3. How many grips are used to create a cross-section corner type cross section?

    a. 1

    b. 2

    c. 3

    d. 4

4. Which of the following Properties can be controlled in the Cross-Section dialog box? (Select all that apply.)

    a. Outline display

    b. Grip display

    c. Grip color

    d. Cross-section visibility

5. By default, the grip for a new cross-section is added at the center of the selected object.

   a. True

   b. False

6. Which of the following Shot Types enables you to create a shot with movement? (Select all that apply.)

   a. Still

   b. Cinematic

   c. Start to end

7. All of the **Shot** swatches that are listed in the Shots interface can be played at the same time.

   a. True

   b. False

8. Which of the following are valid methods of changing the pivot's orientation for a Turntable behavior?

   a. Enter X,Y,Z values in the Turntable Properties dialog box.

   b. Drag the pivot by selecting it in the viewport.

   c. Select the **Rotisserie** option.

   d. The pivot location cannot be modified and must rotate on the floor of the environment.

9. Which of the following transformations can be captured with a Keyframe Animation Behavior? (Select all that apply.)

   a. Positional location on the floor.

   b. Rotational location relative to the floor.

   c. Color changes between alternatives.

   d. Magnification level of the geometry.

10. The following Presentation components have shortcuts that can be used to access their interfaces. Which of the following can have a shortcut key defined to quickly access each of their views?

    a. Cross-section views

    b. Visibility alternatives

    c. Shots

    d. Behaviors

Command Summary

Interface Component	Access Location
Alternative Lineups	• **Menu Bar:** Story>Alternatives • **Shortcut Key:** <A>
Behaviors	• **Menu Bar:** Story>Behaviors • **Shortcut Key:** <B>
Cross-Sections	• **Menu Bar:** Appearance>Cross-sections • **Shortcut Key:** <X>
Shots	• **Menu Bar:** Story>Camera Shots • **Shortcut Key:** <T> • **Task UI:** Click (Look)> (Shots)

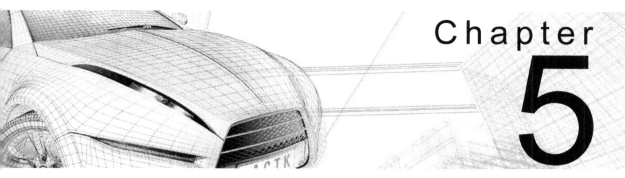

Chapter 5

Presenting a Scene

In this chapter, you learn to create a storyboard by compiling environments, shots, alternatives, and behaviors. You learn to present your model in the form of images, movies, and web presentations. Additionally, you learn to further enhance a presentation by using the Pointer tool to focus on specific areas of a model and how to compare scenes side-by-side.

Learning Objectives in this Chapter

- Create storyboard slides using various alternatives.
- Modify the arrangement of the items in a storyboard and play the slides.
- Create an image of the current view of the scene.
- Create movies and web presentation movies from shots and slides and publish them.
- Identify an area of focus on a model.
- Compare two scenes by placing them side-by-side.

Autodesk Showcase Workflow

Figure 5–1 shows the overall suggested workflow for the Autodesk® Showcase® software. The horizontal line at the top represents the high-level workflow and each of their sub-steps are detailed vertically below them. The highlighted column represents the content discussed in the current chapter.

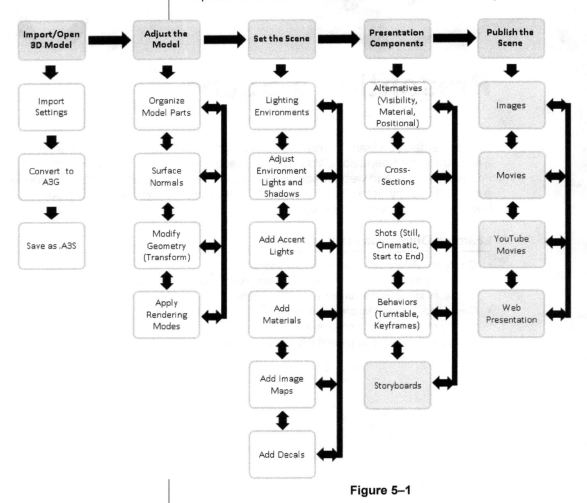

Figure 5–1

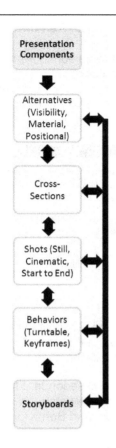

5.1 Storyboard

Storyboarding is a common technique used to graphically represent a sequence of steps that are to be presented to an audience. When published, the storyboard can be used to create images or animated so that all of the graphical items are included in a movie.

To effectively present a design in the Autodesk Showcase software you can combine individual items (alternatives, shots, behaviors, and environments) into a slide. The slides define the storyboard or narrative that is to be conveyed in the presentation. Multiple slides can be created to define the storyboard. Storyboards are created and managed using the Storyboard interface, as shown in Figure 5–2.

Figure 5–2

How To: Create Storyboard Slides

1. Open the Storyboard interface by pressing <U> or selecting **Story>Storyboard**.
2. In the Storyboard interface, click **Create** and select **Storyboard Slide**. An empty slide is added as shown in Figure 5–3.

Figure 5–3

- A checkmark in the bottom left corner indicates that the slide is current.
- You can also open a new empty slide from an existing slide in the interface. Right-click on the existing slide and select **Insert**.

Multiple alternatives, behaviors, and shots can be added to a slide. Only one environment can be added.

3. Double-click on Slide 1 or right-click and select **Rename** to enter a relevant name for the slide.
4. Open the interface from which you want to select an item (alternatives, shots, behaviors, or environment). Right-click on the item that you want to add and select **Add to Current Storyboard Slide**, as shown for an Environment and Shot in Figure 5–4.

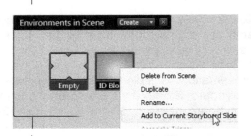 

Figure 5–4

- Once items have been added to a slide, ◀ displays in the right corner of the slide swatch, as shown in Figure 5–5. It expands and compresses the list of items in the slide.

- By default, the time duration of a slide is 3.0 seconds. This displays in the lower right corner of the slide swatch, as shown in Figure 5–5. When you add Shots and Behavior items to the slide, their durations are included in the displayed time. You can change the duration by right-clicking and selecting **Change Duration** or by double-clicking on the duration value and entering a new value.

Figure 5–5

- Use the additional right-click options as required. For example, you can use the **Set Image** option to set a relevant image in the slide swatch.

Slide Properties

In the Storyboard interface, right-click on a slide swatch and select **Properties** to open the Slide Properties dialog box, as shown in Figure 5–6. You can also open the current slide's properties by selecting **Story>Slide Properties**. The dialog box displays all of the items included in the slide and enables you to modify how the items are played in the slide.

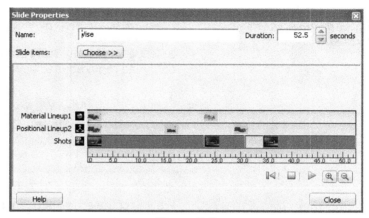

Figure 5–6

Name	Assigns the name of the slide.
Duration	Defines the duration of the slide in seconds.
Slide items	Adds items to the slide. Click **Choose>>** and select items to add to the slide. Items that are already included are grayed out.
Time Line area	Controls the location of the items that have been added to a slide. Drag or enter values to locate the items and arrange them on the timeline.
⏮	Resets to the start of the timeline.
▷ ‖	Plays and pauses the complete slide.
◻	Stops the playing of the slide.

Playing the Slides

Press <Tab> to toggle between Presentation mode and Edit mode.

Once created, individual slides can be played or multiple slides can be played sequentially.

- To play each slide individually, in the Storyboard interface, right-click on the required slide swatch and select **Play Slide From Start**.

- In the Presentation mode, select a slide to play it individually. Press <Esc> to stop playing the slides.

- Select **Story>Play Storyboard Slide** and then select the option as required, as shown in Figure 5–7.

Figure 5–7

- Play all of the slides sequentially using the **Playback** icons in the Storyboard interface title bar, as shown in Figure 5–8.

Figure 5–8

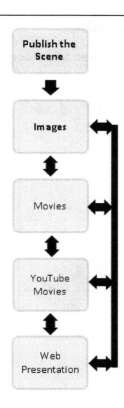

5.2 Publishing

There are different ways to publish your scene and make it available to an audience. These include the following:

- **Images:** Create a high resolution image of an important view of the scene.

- **Movies:** Create movies by compiling shots or slides from a storyboard.

- **YouTube Movies:** Create movies from shots or slides to publish them to YouTube.

- **Web Presentation:** Create a Web presentation from the slides in a storyboard.

All of the publications are generated using the Publish dialog boxes. Tabs along the top of the dialog box provide specific access for each publication type. The title of the dialog box changes depending on the active tab. To open a Publish dialog box, use the **Publish** options in the **File** menu or using the option in the Publish Task UI, as shown on the right in Figure 5–9.

Figure 5–9

If there are no slides or shots in a scene you cannot publish a movie, YouTube video, or web presentation. Additionally, if there are no slides in a scene, a web presentation cannot be created. Movies and YouTube videos can only be created from shots, but web presentations require a slide.

Common Options for All Publish Dialog Boxes

The publishing options that are common between all publication types are highlighted in Figure 5–10.

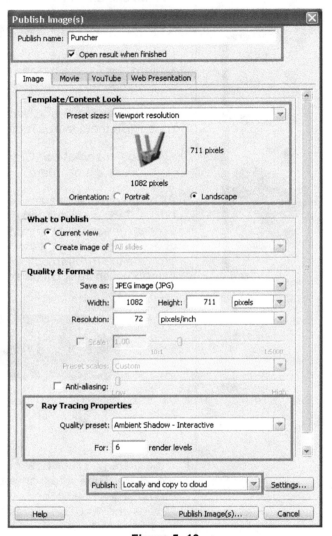

Figure 5–10

Publish name	Assigns the name of the image or movie.
Open result when finished	Controls whether the resulting image displays or if a movie is played after being created.
Template/Content Look	Defines the required output size and orientation of the published image or video.

Ray Tracing Properties	Sets the Ray Tracing properties if the Ray Tracing rendering mode is set as the Visual Style display. Set the preset quality, and set the render levels from 1 to 40 to control the smoothness of the final ray traced rendering. 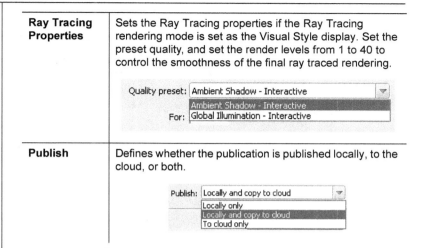
Publish	Defines whether the publication is published locally, to the cloud, or both.

Hint: Publish to Cloud

Autodesk A360 enables you to store, share, and view your content online. You can access your content from anywhere or at anytime by signing into your A360 account. The account can be created at http://360.autodesk.com. Set *Publish* to **To cloud only** or **Locally and copy to cloud** to save your output (image or movie) to Autodesk 360.

Publishing Images

Select **File>Publish Image(s)** or click ⬚ (Publish)>

⬚ (Image) in the Task UI to open the Publish Image(s) dialog box. The options that are specific to image publishing are shown in Figure 5–11.

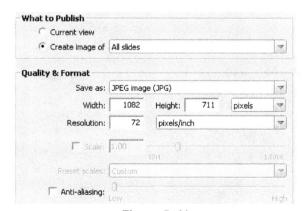

Figure 5–11

What to Publish	Creates an image of the current viewport or select different slides or shots whose images you want to create.
Save as	Defines the file format for the image being published. The options include **JPEG**, **TIFF**, **TIFF HDR**, **BMP**, **PSD**, and **HDR**. **Note -** When publishing TIFF files, you have the option to use the alpha channel to isolate an object. Select **Add Alpha (to isolate object)** to add the alpha channel. **Note -** When publishing PSD files, you have the option to split objects, shadows, and environments into separate layers (**Split into object, shadow and environment layers**) in addition to being able to control transparent objects. By toggling the **No Alpha for transparent objects in object layer**, you can control transparency against the image background.
Width, Height, Resolution	Displays the width, height, and resolution of the image being published. These values are based on the selected preset size in the *Template/Content Look* area. If **Custom** is selected, you can set specific dimensions and resolutions.
Scale	Sets an accurate scale and adjusts the zoom of the image. This option is only available for orthographic views.
Anti-Aliasing	Controls the edge smoothness in the published image. Once enabled, use the slider bar to adjust the quality. This does not dynamically affect the viewport, the use of anti-aliasing is only displayed in the published image.

Publishing Movies

Select **File>Publish Movie(s)** or click 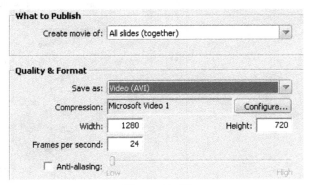 (Publish)>

(Movie) in the Task UI, to open the Publish Movie(s) dialog box. The options that are specific to creating a movie are shown in Figure 5–12.

If using a 64bit Autodesk Showcase installation, you cannot create movies using a 32bit codec.

What to Publish

Create movie of: All slides (together)

Quality & Format

Save as: Video (AVI)

Compression: Microsoft Video 1   Configure...

Width: 1280   Height: 720

Frames per second: 24

Anti-aliasing: Low   High

Figure 5–12

What to Publish	Enables you to create a single movie of all of the created shots or slides, separate movies of individual shots and slides, or a combination of single or separate movies of selected shots and slides.
Save as	Defines the file format for the movie being published. The options include **AVI**, **JPEG**, **TIFF**, **HDR**, and other formats, such as FLV, MP4, MOV, and Web Movie.
Compression	Enables you to set the AVI codec. The options available depend on your system.
Width/Height	Defines the height and width of the movie being published. These values are based on the selected preset size in the *Template/Content Look* area. Enter new values to customize the size.
Frames per second	Defines the frames per second setting that is used when the movie is published.
Anti-aliasing	Controls the edge smoothness in the published image. Once enabled, use the slider bar to adjust the quality. This does not dynamically affect the viewport, anti-aliasing is only displayed in the published image.

Publishing YouTube Movies

Select **File>Publish to YouTube** or click (Publish)> (YouTube) in the Task UI to open the Publish to YouTube dialog box. It is similar to the Publish to movie(s) dialog box. The only difference is that no compression is permitted when publishing to Youtube.

- You need to have a YouTube account to publish a movie to YouTube.

Publishing Web Presentations

Select **File>Publish Web Presentation** or click 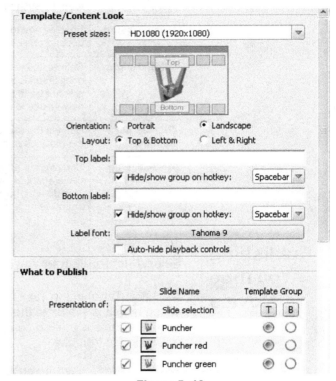 (Publish)> (Web) in the Task UI to open the Publish Presentation dialog box. Options that are specific to web presentations are shown in Figure 5–13.

Figure 5–13

Layout	Controls where the thumbnails of the slide images are placed: horizontally along the **Top & Bottom** or vertically along the **Left & Right**.
Label and Label font	Enter a group name for the top slides or bottom slides. You can also set the font for these labels.
What to Publish	Sets the slides that are placed in the **T** (Top) or **B** (Bottom) groups for the **Top & Bottom** Layout, or the slides that are placed along the **L** (Left) or **R** (Right) groups for the **Left & Right** Layout. You can also control which slides to include or exclude from the publication.
Save as	Defines the file format for the web presentation being published. The options include **HTML** or **Flash** (JPEG images or FLV).

5.3 Pointer Tool

While presenting a scene you can identify an area of focus using the **Pointer** tool. Once the **Pointer** tool has been enabled, the overall scene is grayed out except for a circular white area (similar to a spot light) that is used to identify the focus area. The focus area can be moved and scaled, as required.

How To: Use a Pointer

1. Select **Present>Pointer** or press <P>. The scene is grayed out and a white spot displays, as shown in Figure 5–14.

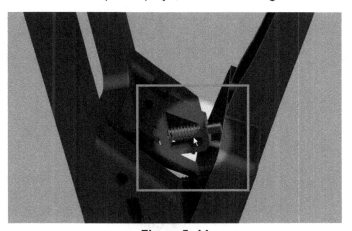

Figure 5–14

2. Hold <P> and move the cursor (without clicking) to reposition the pointer (white spot) on the model. Release <P> when the cursor is at the required area of focus.
3. Increase or decrease the size of the pointer (white spot) by holding <P> and using the mouse wheel. Alternatively, while holding <P>, click the left mouse button and move the cursor. Release <P> when the cursor is the required size.
4. Press <P> again or press <Esc> to exit the **Pointer** tool.

When holding <P> and using the mouse wheel, you can also move the cursor to reposition the area of focus at the same time.

5.4 Compare Scenes

The Compare Scenes interface enables you to place two similar models side-by-side to compare or contrast their design features. To compare scenes, two scenes should already be saved.

How To: Compare Scenes

1. Select **Present>Compare Scenes** or press <C>. The Compare Scene interface opens with the current scene swatch displayed, as shown in Figure 5–15. Note that ▬ (Eye) displays in the lower left corner, indicating that it is the currently active scene.

Figure 5–15

2. In the Compare Scene interface, click **AddScene**. A warning dialog box opens, prompting you that once multiple scenes have been loaded, changes cannot be saved. Click **Continue**.
3. The Add Scene dialog box opens. Browse to the location of the scene to be compared and open it.
4. The new scene opens in the viewport and its swatch displays in the Compare Scene interface, as shown in Figure 5–16.

   Note that ▬ (Eye) displays in the new scene, indicating that it is now the currently active scene.

Figure 5–16

5. Select either scene swatch to display it in the current viewport.

The active scene displays on the left when the side-by-side presentation has been set.

6. Select **Present>Side-by-Side**. The scenes display next to each another, as shown in Figure 5–17.

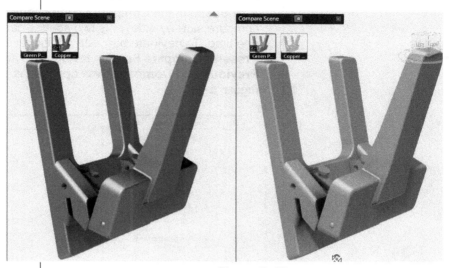

Figure 5–17

7. Orbit, Pan, or Zoom the model. Note that both scenes change in the same way, enabling model comparison.As an alternative you can also compare Shots. In Figure 5–18, the orientation and zoom level are the same for both scenes.

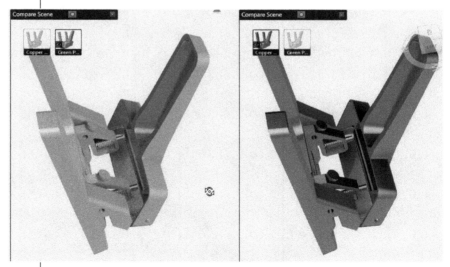

Figure 5–18

8. Select **Present>Side-by-Side** to disable the side-by-side display. You cannot save changes made while comparing.

Hint: Loading Multiple Scenes

More than two scenes can be loaded for comparison by clicking **Add Scene** in the Compare Scene interface. When set to compare side-by-side, only two scenes can be compared at one time. To navigate between additional scenes, select **Present>Compare Scenes Navigation** and use the **Compare Previous** and **Compare Next** options, as shown in Figure 5–19.

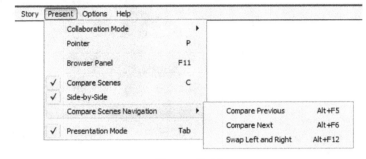

Figure 5–19

Practice 5a

Creating Storyboard Slides

Practice Objectives

- Create storyboard slides using alternative items and shots.
- Modify the arrangement of the items and play the created slides.

In this practice you will create a storyboard slide using different alternatives items and shots. You will then modify the arrangement of the items using the Storyboard Properties dialog box. You will finally play the created slides.

Estimated time for completion: 25 minutes

Task 1 - Creating storyboard slides.

1. Click 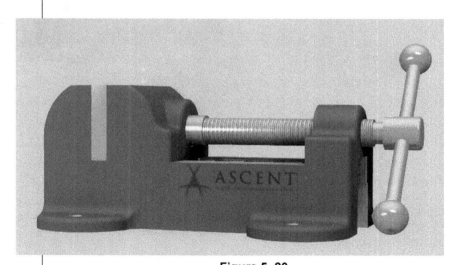 (Your File) in the (Open File) Task UI or select **File>Open**.

*The **Empty** environment was used for clarity in printing the images. Your model display will be different*

2. In the Open File dialog box, browse to the *Vise_Presentation* folder of your practice files folder. Open **Vise_Presentation.a3s**. A 3D model of a vise in the ID Bloom environment displays, similar to that shown in Figure 5–20.

Figure 5–20

3. Open the Storyboard interface by pressing <U> or selecting **Story>Storyboard**.

4. If the accent light or decal grip display in the scene, clear the required grip option in the **Options** menu.

---

5. In the Storyboard interface, click **Create** and select **Storyboard Slide**. An empty slide swatch (shown in Figure 5–21), is created in the interface. Note the checkmark at the lower left corner indicating that the swatch is active.

6. Right-click on the swatch and select **Rename**. Type **Vise Design** as the slide name, as shown in Figure 5–22.

Figure 5–21   Figure 5–22

7. Press <E> to open the Environments interface. Note that three environments are listed in the *Environments in Scene* interface. The ID Bloom environment is active.

8. Right-click on the **ID SimpleSkylight** swatch and select **Add to Current Storyboard Slide**, as shown in Figure 5–23.

Figure 5–23

- Note that ◄ displays near the upper right side of the **Vise Design** slide swatch followed by the **ID SimpleSkylight** swatch, as shown in Figure 5–24.

9. Right-click on the **Vise Design** slide swatch and select **Set Image** to set the current viewport as the slide image, as shown in Figure 5–25.

The environment listed in the slide is used while the slide is played regardless of the current active environment.

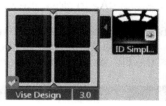

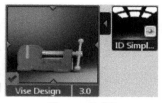

Figure 5–24   **Figure 5–25**

10. Select **Story>Alternatives** or press <A> to open the Alternative Lineups interface. A Material and Positional lineup have already been created in the file (use the arrow to display all the lineups and swatches), as shown in Figure 5–26.

11. In *Material Lineup1*, right-click on Anodized red and select **Add to Current Storyboard Slide**, as shown in Figure 5–27. Note that the **Anodized red** swatch is added to the Vise Design slide.

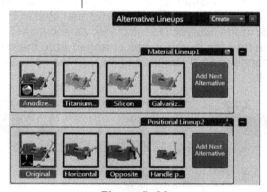

Figure 5–26   **Figure 5–27**

12. In *Material Lineup1*, right-click on Titanium polished and select **Add to Current Storyboard Slide**.

13. From *Positional Lineup2*, add the **Original**, **Horizontal**, and **Handle pulled** items to the Vise Design slide. Note that all of the added items are listed in the Vise Design slide in the Storyboard interface, as shown in Figure 5–28.

Figure 5–28

14. Press <A> to close the Alternatives Lineup interface.

15. Select **Story>Camera Shots** or press <T> to open the Shots interface. A number of shots have already been created in the file, as shown in Figure 5–29.

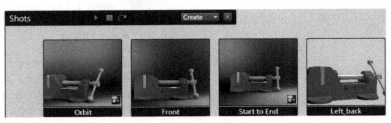

Figure 5–29

Items in a slide can be repositioned by selecting and dragging them to a new position in the storyboard slide.

16. In the Shots interface, add the **Orbit**, **Left_back**, and **Start to End** items to the Vise Design slide by right-clicking on the required shot swatch and selecting **Add to Current Storyboard Slide**. Ensure that you add them in the listed sequence. All of the added items are listed in the Vise Design slide in the Storyboard interface, as shown in Figure 5–30. Note that the Duration has changed from the default 3.0 seconds to **53.0** seconds to include the time duration of the shots.

Figure 5–30

17. Close the Shots interface.

18. In the Storyboard interface, click **Create** and select **Storyboard Slide** to create another empty slide. Rename it to **Standing**.

19. Press <E> to open the Environments interface.

20. Add the ID Bloom environment to the *Standing* slide by right-clicking on ID Bloom and selecting **Add to Current Storyboard Slide**.

You can open the Alternative Lineups by pressing <A>.

*Select **Story>Camera Shots** or press <T> to open the Shots interface.*

21. In the Alternative Lineups interface, in *Material Lineup1*, select **Silicon** to make it active. Note that in the viewport the material of the vise changes to **Silicon**. Set the current viewport as the image for the **Standing** slide swatch (right-click>**Set Image**), as shown in Figure 5–31.

22. Add **Silicon** to the *Standing* storyboard slide.

23. In the Shots interface, add **Front** to the Standing slide. The items in the Standing slide display as shown in Figure 5–32.

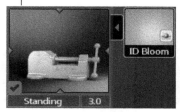
Figure 5–31

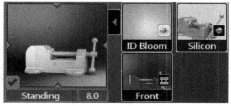
Figure 5–32

24. Close the Alternative Lineups and Shots interfaces, if not already closed.

Task 2 - Arranging items in the slide.

---

1. In the Storyboard interface, right-click on the **Vise Design** slide swatch and select **Properties** to open the Slide Properties dialog box as shown in Figure 5–33.

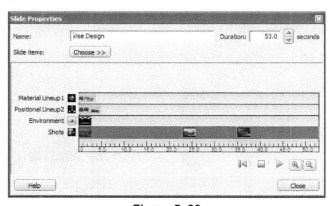
Figure 5–33

- Note that all of the items are listed in the *Timeline* area. Only the items in the *Shots* row are located at specific times in the sequence. This is based on the time specified for each shot. Their sequence is based on the sequence in which they were added to the Vise Design slide.

---

2. In the *Timeline* area, in the *Shots* row, hover the cursor over the first item swatch. It displays the name and highlights the time duration of this shot, as shown in Figure 5–34. This indicates that it is the Orbit shot and that its duration is 23.0 seconds.

Figure 5–34

3. In the *Shots* row, select the blue area after the second swatch. In addition to displaying the time duration, a gray vertical bar displays indicating the starting point of the shot, as shown in Figure 5–35. This means that the shot plays from 23.0 seconds to 35.0 seconds.

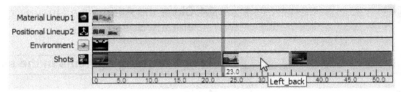

Figure 5–35

4. Right-click on the highlighted area for **Left_back** (the secon shot) and select **Properties**, as shown on the left in Figure 5–36. The Shot Properties dialog box opens as shown on the right in Figure 5–36.

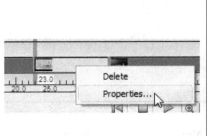

Figure 5–36

5. In the Shot Properties dialog box, set the *Duration* to **10.0** seconds.

6. Close the Shot Properties dialog box. Note that in the Slide Properties dialog box, the **Left_back** duration has extended to 37.0 seconds (from 35.0), as shown in Figure 5–37.

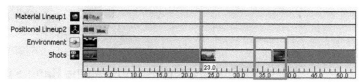

Figure 5–37

7. In the Slide Properties dialog box, in the *Timeline* area, in the *Material Lineup1* row, note that two items are overlapping each other. The left is the Anodized red and the right is Titanium polished name.

8. Click and drag the **Titanium polished** item (right side one) swatch and place it at approximately **30.0** seconds in the timeline, as shown in Figure 5–38. This changes the material of the vise from *Anodized red* to *Titanium polished* at the 30.0 seconds mark of the slide.

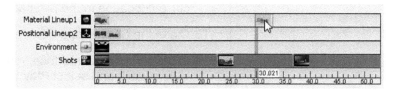

Figure 5–38

9. Review the items in the *Positional Lineup2* row. There are three items **Original**, **Horizontal**, and **Handle pulled** as shown in Figure 5–39.

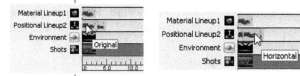 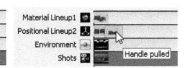

Figure 5–39

10. Click and drag the **Horizontal (middle)** item swatch and place it at approximately the **20.0** seconds location on the timeline, as shown in Figure 5–40.

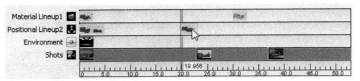

Figure 5–40

11. Click and drag the **Handle pulled (right)** item swatch and place it at approximately the **40.0** seconds location on the timeline, as shown in Figure 5–41.

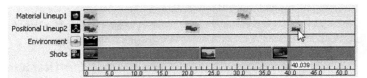

Figure 5–41

12. Click ▷ to play the story board in the viewport. The gray progress bar displays in the *Timeline* area, indicating the current location in the playback.

13. Close the Slide Properties dialog box.

14. In the Storyboard interface, right-click on the **Vise Design** slide swatch and select **Play Slide From Start**. The playback begins again in the viewport.

15. In the Storyboard title bar, click ▶ to play both slides sequentially. Note how the environment changes as the playback switches between slides.

16. Save your scene as **MyVise_Presentation.a3s** in the *Vise_Presentation* folder of your practice files folder.

Practice 5b

Estimated time for completion: 10 minutes

The Empty environment was used for clarity in printing the image. Your model display will be different.

Publishing Images and Movies

Practice Objective

- Create images and a movie from shots and slides.

In this practice you will create images and movies from the created shots and slides.

Task 1 - Creating images and movies.

1. Click ![icon] (Your File) in the ![icon] (Open File) Task UI or select **File>Open**.

2. In the Open File dialog box, browse to the *Vise_Movies* folder of your practice files folder and open **Vise_Movies.a3s**. A 3D model of a vise in the ID Bloom environment displays, as shown in Figure 5–42.

Figure 5–42

3. Select **File>Publish Image(s)** to open the Publish Image(s) dialog box.

4. In the *What to Publish* area, select **Create image of**, expand the drop-down list, and select **Shot selection**, as shown on the left in Figure 5–43. The list of created shots displays. Clear the **Left_back** option and keep the rest selected as shown on the right in Figure 5–43.

Figure 5–43

5. At the bottom of the dialog box, set *Publish* to **Locally only**. Set the remaining options (*Width* to **1082**; *Height* to **711**) as shown in Figure 5–44.

*If you want to share your images, set Publish to **To cloud only** or **Locally and copy to cloud** to save your output (image or movie) to A360.*

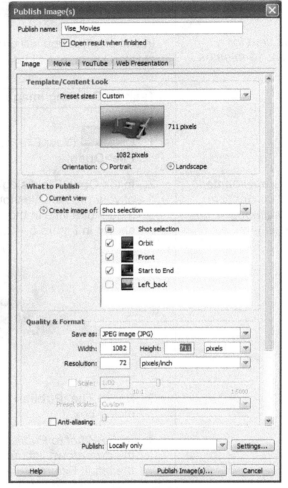

Figure 5–44

6. Click Publish Image(s). The Save Image As dialog box opens.

7. In your practice files folder, browse to the *Vise_Movies* folder. Note that the default filename of **Vise_Movies.jpg** displays. Click **Save**.

8. The first image displays in the photo viewer because **Open result when finished** was selected in the Publish Image(s) dialog box. Close the photo viewer.

9. Using Windows Explorer, browse to your practice files folder, and the *Vise_Movies* folder. Note that three image files (**Vise_Movies_Front.jpg**, **Vise_Movies_Orbit.jpg**, and **Vise_Movies_StartToEnd.jpg**) have been created. There is one for each selected shot, as shown in Figure 5–45.

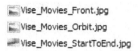

Figure 5–45

You can select the YouTube tab, create a movie, and publish it to YouTube.

10. In the Autodesk Showcase software, select **File>Publish Image(s)** to open the Publish Image(s) dialog box.

11. Select the *Movie* tab to display the Publish Movie(s) dialog box. Alternatively, you can select **File>Publish Movie(s)** to automatically open the dialog box with the correct tab open.

12. In the *What to Publish* area, expand the Create movie of drop-down list and select **Slide selection (separate)**. Clear the **Standing** option and verify that the other options in the dialog box are as shown in Figure 5–46.

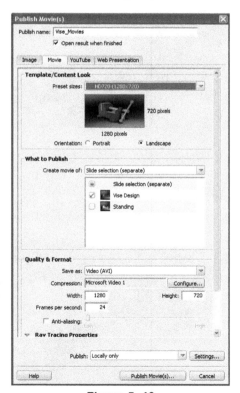

Figure 5–46

13. Click **Publish Movie(s)...**. The Save Movie As dialog box opens.

14. In your practice files folder, browse to the *Vise_Movies* folder. Note that a default filename of **Vise_Movies.avi** displays. Click **Save**. Note that it can take a few minutes to create the movie.

15. In your practice files folder, open the *Vise_Movies* folder. Note that **Vise_Movies_slide1.avi** has been created.

16. Double-click on **Vise_Movies_slide1.avi** to play the movie. Use the player controls to review the movie. Then, close the player.

17. Close the scene without saving.

Chapter Review Questions

1. Which of the following statements are true regarding the storyboard in an Autodesk Showcase file? (Select all that apply.)

   a. The duration of a behavior item in a storyboard slide must be manually added to the slide duration to reflect its correct duration in the overall slide duration.

   b. Items that have been added to a storyboard slide cannot be added a second time to the same slide.

   c. While in Presentation mode, you can select a slide to play it. You do not need to use the playback controls.

   d. Only a single storyboard slide can be played at a time.

2. Multiple alternatives, behaviors, shots, and environments can be added to a storyboard slide.

   a. True

   b. False

3. Which of the following publication types are not available if no slides exist in a scene? (Select all that apply.)

   a. Images

   b. Movies

   c. YouTube

   d. Web Presentations

4. Which of the following best describes how to move the **Pointer** tool's area of focus in a scene? (Select all that apply.)

   a. Hold <P> and the left mouse button while moving the cursor.

   b. Hold <P> and scroll the mouse wheel while moving the cursor.

   c. Hold <P> and move the cursor.

   d. Press and release <P>.

5. When scenes are added for comparison, the **Zoom** navigation tool only affects the scene that was active before they were displayed side-by-side.

   a. True

   b. False

Command Summary

Interface Component	Access Location
Compare Scenes	• **Menu Bar:** Present>Compare Scenes • **Shortcut Key:** <C>
Pointer	• **Menu Bar:** Present>Pointer • **Shortcut Key:** <P>
Publish options (*Image, Movie, YouTube, and Web Presentation*)	• **Task UI:** Click (Publish)> (Image), (Movie), (YouTube), or (Web Presentation) • **Menu Bar:** File>Publish Image(s), Publish Movie(s), Publish to YouTube, or Publish Web Presentation.
Side-by-Side	• **Menu Bar:** Present>Side-by-Side
Storyboard	• **Menu Bar:** Story>Storyboard • **Shortcut Key:** <U>

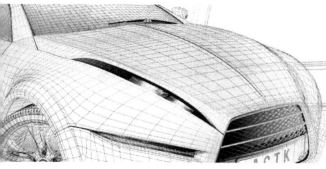

Index

www.ingramcontent.com/pod-product-compliance
Lightning Source LLC
Chambersburg PA
CBHW060542060326
40690CB00017B/3576